CATOCTIN FURNACE

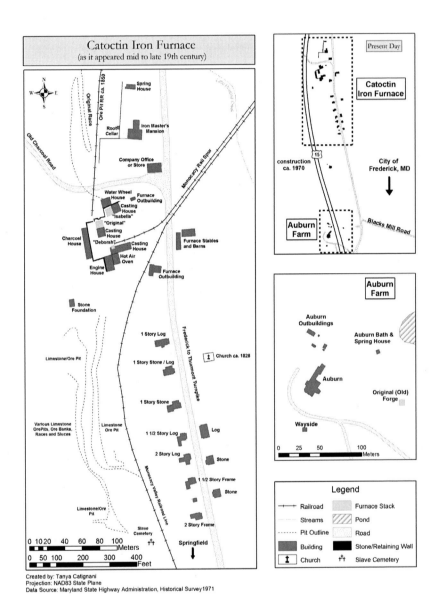

Mid- to late nineteenth-century appearance of the Catoctin Furnace village, with detail of Auburn Farm. *Created by Tanya Catignania.*

CATOCTIN FURNACE

PORTRAIT OF AN IRON-MAKING VILLAGE

ELIZABETH YOURTEE ANDERSON

EDITED BY ELIZABETH ANDERSON COMER

Charleston  London

THE
History
PRESS

Published by The History Press
Charleston, SC 29403
www.historypress.net

Front cover, top: *Deborah Furnace in Blast* by Claudette Pridemore, 1975, oil on canvas. *Bottom*: Photograph of Isabella stack and casting shed, Catoctin Furnace, by Cam Miller, 2012.

Back cover: Photograph of circa 1810 double log house, headquarters of the Catoctin Furnace Historical Society, by Cam Miller, 2012.

First published 2013

Manufactured in the United States

ISBN 978.1.62619.001.6

Library of Congress CIP data applied for.

CONTENTS

PREFACE

EDITOR'S NOTE: *Researching and writing Catoctin Furnace: Portrait of an Iron-Making Village was a true labor of love for my mother. As a social historian, her goal was to produce a collective biography of the furnace workers and to give them a voice so their lifework and contribution to the success of industry in the United States would not be overlooked. Her painstaking research continued until her death in 2011, and it was her dream to see this book in print. In the original manuscript, she ended the story when the furnace shut down for the final time. She and I talked about adding a chapter that covered the preservation movement in the twentieth century, and this has been done. I have had the help of family and friends: I am indebted to Margaret and Jacob Comer for reading and editing the manuscript, to Anne Comer for helping interpret village life, to Joel Anderson for contributing the chapter on the mechanics of the furnace, to Robert Wanner and Tery Harris for help with the manuscript and to Chris Gardiner and Laura Gardiner for help with images. Finally, a thank you goes to the members of the Catoctin Furnace Historical Society, Inc., who keep the spirit and heritage of Catoctin Furnace alive. What follows is my mother's original preface to this work.*

My fascination with Catoctin Furnace reaches back to a memory of well-proportioned, neatly whitewashed houses clustered along the road between Frederick and Thurmont, Maryland. I had heard stories of the involvement of Maryland's first governor, Thomas Johnson, with the old iron furnace. An air of romance surrounded the place. The frantic hustle and din of the past were quiet, and the ironmaster's mansion seemed to sleep in the serenity. Years later, when I returned to the Thurmont area and began to attend Harriet Chapel, my curiosity about the history of Catoctin Furnace was reawakened. I was delighted to be able to buy one of the workers' cottages and, along with my family, plan and execute its restoration.

PREFACE

When the opportunity arose to work on an honors paper, I was encouraged to choose Catoctin Furnace as the subject. My first reaction was that most of the information had already been uncovered. The furnace was mentioned in historical accounts such as Scharf's *History of Western Maryland* and Williams's *History of Frederick County*. Also, a number of archaeological investigations had taken place in the area, each of which had included historical research. My fears about a lack of information were completely unfounded. There was a wealth of undiscovered material on Catoctin Furnace. I have spent eight months in research and realize that there are records and stories I have not uncovered. The search will go on.

The people who have helped me in my research are too numerous to mention. I particularly want to thank Marie Burns, who gently helped me find my way through a tangle of land transfers; Clement and Harriet Gardiner, who put up with my presence for days as I read hundreds of pages of letters and ledgers; Joanne Miller, who made copies; members of the Catoctin Furnace Historical Society Eugene Anderson, Mary Rae Cantwell and William Renner; members of the Anders, Carbaugh, Fraley, Hoke, Martin, Miller, Penwell, Reed, Stitely and Sweeney families of the Catoctin Furnace area; the priest and people of Catoctin Episcopal Parish, whose interest and encouragement meant so much; the staff of C. Burr Artz Library; the Washington County library staff; Moravian Archives personnel, including my translator, Robert Steelman; the Episcopal Diocese of Maryland's Garner Ranney, archivist; Kay Harbaugh and Judith Ricketts of the Board of Education of Frederick County; and Tanya Catignani, for producing the site map. John McGrain provided valuable editing and additional Catoctin Furnace references from his extensive files.

Everywhere I went I was treated most courteously. The staffs of the Library of Congress, National Archives, Maryland Hall of Records, Eleutherian Mills Historical Library, Maryland Historical Society and Frederick County Courthouse were very helpful. I feel that the material I have gathered has been the result of a joint effort. I could not have done it alone. I especially want to thank Dr. Leonard Latkovski and Dr. Gerald McKnight, advisors, whose guidance and patience are deeply appreciated.

This research could never have been accomplished if it had not been for the support of my family—especially Elizabeth Anderson Comer, for her companionship, help and advice, and Joel Anderson, for his help and interest as "official photographer" and for his patience. I have been researching and writing of the past, but I want to dedicate my work to the future, so that the story may live for the younger generation as it has come to life for me. In that spirit, I dedicate this book to Margaret, Jacob, Anne, Kate, Kelby, Chaslyn, Caleb, Jeffrey, Derek, Adrienne and Lilienne.

Chapter 1

THE EARLY YEARS

Thomas Johnson and his brother James located their iron furnace in an area that had shown earlier promise as an industrial site. The builders found all the necessary elements for a successful operation on the eastern slope of Catoctin Mountain in northern Frederick County, Maryland. Their choice proved to be a wise one, for Catoctin Furnace would operate for over a century. Not only were they establishing a business, but the Johnsons were also deeply involved in the American Revolution.

Pioneers came to the central lands of provincial Maryland for a number of reasons. Some hoped to settle and operate small businesses. Others were speculators, like the Johnsons, bent on development and industrialization. Some followed trails leading from Pennsylvania settlements to new lands farther south. Others pushed west from Maryland's Tidewater.

Early arrivals to the area were attracted not only by the rich land but also by clear rushing streams and a plentiful supply of timber. Abundant water, needed by the settlers for crops and livestock, was also a source of power. Logs, used for building and shaped into tools and furniture, were also a vital source of fuel.

Under the provisions of the Charter of Maryland, the Lord Proprietary owned all the land in the province, with power to grant any part of it to someone willing to pay an annual rent. In March 1732, Lord Baltimore, hoping to attract German settlers from Pennsylvania, offered a tract to any person who would settle on the back land of the province. One of the earliest settlers to take advantage of this offer was John Vertrees (Verdies),

Thomas Johnson (1732–1819) at the age of thirty-six, first governor of Maryland, developer of the Catoctin Furnace. *Painting by John Hesselius, now in the U.S. Supreme Court Building.*

who received a patent on December 13, 1738, for 128 acres, which he named John's Mountain.[1] Vertrees's land was well situated on the eastern slope of Catockton (Catoctin) Mountain, "beginning at a bounded Black Oak standing at the head of a spring on the west side of Hunting Creek about fifty or sixty perches above a mirey lique."[2]

Joining Vertrees in this region known in early days as Monoquice (Monocacy) or "The Turckey" were other families, most of German origin.[3]

Among them was Hans Martin Wetzel and his family, who had arrived on September 21, 1731.[4] The Wetzels became squatters in the area for several years before receiving a patent on October 1, 1741, for one hundred acres of land. This tract, known as Mill Place, began "at a bounded white oak standing on the east side of Little Hunting Creek near the lower end of a small island in the said creek."[5]

Mills were an integral part of life in the Monocacy area. In addition to the mill on Little Hunting Creek at Mill Place, Vertrees had a sawmill on John's Mountain, selling poplar lumber.[6] Construction and maintenance of these mills required a certain amount of forge and blacksmith work. At a very early date, a forge was operating near Vertrees's sawmill.[7] It is reasonable to assume that concentrated activity and growing industrialization in the area made the settlers aware of the presence of iron ore on the slopes of the John's Mountain tract and influenced others to purchase and speculate.

As settlement spread, the provincial government encouraged responses to the pressing need for iron. In order to make industrial development more attractive, an act was passed in the Maryland legislature in 1719 offering one hundred acres of land to anyone who would establish an iron furnace or forge in the province.[8] In 1722, laborers in the iron industry were exempted from mending public roads and later were exempted from militia duties.[9]

Another major factor in the growth of the colonial iron industry was England's inability to produce enough pig iron to meet the demands of its industry. English forests, necessary for the burning of charcoal, were becoming scarce. Manufacturing interests pressed for colonial iron to supply their needs.

Men with business and industrial interests were aware of the potential profit to be realized from iron making. An iron furnace had been set up on Principio Creek in Cecil County in 1723 by a group of wealthy English ironmasters and merchants.[10] Among those watching their success was Dr. Charles Carroll of Annapolis. Carroll and his associates began to patent tracts that were potential sites for furnaces. In 1752, he acquired "Good Will," 150 acres "beside of John's Mountain,"[11] and "Stoney Park, northerly from the dwelling of John Vertrees,"[12] further indication of awareness of the presence of iron ore in the area.

Hampton Furnace was built on one of Dr. Carroll's tracts on Tom's Creek, one and a half miles west of Emmitsburg. Operating in the early 1760s, Hampton lacked a supply of good ore. In order to use the furnace that had been constructed there, ore was hauled from deposits on the tracts at Catoctin.[13] This was not a practical operation because transportation was slow and difficult. It would have been far better to locate the furnace close to the source of ore. Power was available from the waters of Little Hunting Creek. Also, the Catoctin Mountain was an excellent source of wood for charcoal, and there were limestone deposits slightly east of the mountain.[14]

One of Dr. Carroll's associates, the Annapolis attorney Thomas Johnson, had a brief and less-than-successful venture in the iron industry's Green Spring Furnace on Licking Creek.[15] The ore at Green Spring was not rich enough to make that operation profitable, but Johnson did not lose interest and switched his attention to the rich hematite ore deposits at Catoctin. In December 1768, a group of men including Thomas Johnson, Benedict Calvert, John Davidson and James Johnson petitioned the royal governor for a tract of vacant land that came to be known as the Mountain Tract "for the purpose of erecting and building an iron works."[16] The warrant issued to them was not executed until 1770. In the meantime, on March 24, 1769, in partnership with Benedict Calvert, Thomas Johnson purchased John's Mountain from John Valentine Vertrees, who had inherited it at the death of John Vertrees in 1753.[17] The following year, Calvert and Johnson, along with John Davidson and James Johnson, Thomas's brother, renewed the warrant for vacant land. They were granted 7,587 acres, which, added to the 128 acres they had purchased, combined to create a tract of 7,715 acres.[18] Now they had adequate timber resources as well as rich ore deposits and water power.

Thomas Johnson Jr. was the son of Thomas and Dorcas Sedgwick Johnson of Calvert County. As a young man, he had read law in Annapolis and had become a very eminent lawyer. His association with businessmen and politicians of the colonial government provided him with extraordinary opportunities in the emerging nation. Johnson was a close friend of George Washington, with whom he shared an interest in the development of the young land. As Johnson shifted part of his interest to Frederick County, he was joined by three of his brothers. Like Thomas, Baker and Roger Johnson were trained in the law. They also shared Thomas's interest in the infant iron industry. James Johnson was a skilled ironmaster. There is speculation that he learned his trade at Snowden's Ironworks on Little Patuxent River, located near the Johnson family home.[19] When Thomas Johnson became involved in the iron-making venture at Green Spring Furnace, James was the ironmaster. After Green Spring shut down, James moved to Catoctin in November 1774, residing "on the spot where the Auburn House now stands."[20] The next step was to get a furnace built and in blast.

Wayside, a mid-eighteenth-century stone house on the Auburn estate. *Photography courtesy of Joel T. Anderson.*

Within the next year, James Johnson had selected a site and begun construction of the furnace complex. He needed to locate close to Little Hunting Creek. A millpond and raceway had to be built to carry water to turn the great wheel that powered the bellows. The spot that Johnson selected was located on Good Will. In January 1776, Thomas Johnson struck a bargain with Charles Carroll, barrister, to take possession of Good Will and Stoney Park in exchange for one hundred tons of pig iron.[21] The deed transferring the land to the Johnsons was not drawn up until 1803, when Nicholas Carroll passed it to Baker Johnson.[22]

During the Revolution, the Johnsons were staunch Patriots. Maryland was divided into five districts with a brigadier general assigned to each. On January 6, 1776, Thomas Johnson was elected brigadier general of the upper district[23] and was also named senior brigadier general of Maryland.[24] His brothers were also militia men. James and Roger were both attached to the Second Battalion—James as colonel and Roger as second major. Baker Johnson was colonel of the Fourth Battalion.[25]

Due to the fact that they were involved in the iron industry, the Johnsons began to receive inquiries about munitions. On July 15, 1776, the Council of Safety wrote to Colonel James Johnson:

Sir: We are in want of about 20 4 lb. Cannon, 20 3 lb. and 40 swivels for the use of the Province & desire to know whether you will engage to furnish us with those quantities immediately—if you can, be pleased to favor us as soon as possible with your terms and the time by which you will have them made, tho' it will be much more agreeable to see you upon the occasion—We shall likewise want 200 Iron Potts some to contain 4 & others 2 gallons—with Bales or Handles to supply the place of Camp Kettles, and should be glad you would advise us whether you could also cast them for us & by what time—likewise the price.[26]

One week later, on July 22, 1776, Thomas Johnson replied for his brother. James did not have the furnace in blast, he wrote, but was proceeding "with all diligence" and hoped to have it in blast within a fortnight. He also listed some items that they did have on hand: "potts...Kettles and a few Dutch ovens."[27] After the furnace was in blast, he promised that the council could "have any number of pots and kettles...in a short time." With respect to guns, Johnson did not make a definite commitment, fearing that the "metal may not suit." He went on to say:

If we succeed in making good Guns the Public may have them delivered at Baltimore at 40 £ a Ton...If any Body also will contract for a Certainty, I wish he should be preferred even at a greater price.[28]

On that same day, July 22, the council wrote back, commending Johnson on the readiness of the militia of Frederick. The letter continued:

If your Brothers Iron is suitable for casting guns we could contract with you for 50 3 Pounders, 50 4' & 75 Swivels to carry 1 lb Ball—Capt. Nicholson informs us that the length of the swivels is not material—the 3 & 4 pounders ought to be somewhat shorter than the common standard.[29]

When he got his furnace into blast, James Johnson cast a variety of products. In August 1777, he advertised in Dunlap's *Maryland Journal and Baltimore Advertiser*:

Salt-Pans, ten feet square, and fifteen inches deep, with screws ready to join and set them up, made at the Furnace, about 10 miles from Frederick-Town, at fifty-five pounds per ton. If different sizes are desired they will be attempted—Carriage from the furnace to Baltimore, is now at seven pounds a ton. Orders left with Messrs. Lux and Bowley, will be forwarded and duly executed.[30]

Saltpans were used for brine evaporation in the manufacture of salt. James Johnson & Co. also cast stove plates for widely used heating and cooking stoves, fire backs, tools, weights and utensils.[31]

The protracted conflict between England and its colonies prompted the Revolutionary government to enter into a contractual agreement with the Johnsons in the fall of 1780. Captain Daniel Joy, acting for the United States, and James Johnson, acting for himself and his partners at Catoctin Furnace, agreed that the Johnsons would prepare to cast ten-inch shells and, if successful, would cast them until October 15, 1780. These shells were to be shipped by wagon to Baltimore Town and delivered to the Continental quartermaster. All good shells would be paid for at the rate of fifty pounds per ton, one-half to be paid at the delivery of the last parcel of shells and the other half to be paid with interest at 6 percent on October 15, 1781. In addition, one-fourth of the price of the carriage was to be paid to James Johnson and partners at the time of the first payment.[32]

The shells were delivered. David Poe of the Quartermaster Division certified that he took delivery of thirty-one tons, four hundredweight, one-

Above: James Johnson and Co. fire back, dated 1776, in the home of Richard and Dixie Miller. *Photograph courtesy of John T. Anderson.*

Right: A 1786 Johnson and Co. six-plate cast-iron stove. *Photography courtesy of Old Salem, Inc.*

quarter and eighteen pounds of bombshells for ten-inch mortars, the last delivery being on the twentieth day of October 1780, and gave a receipt for each delivery. Further certification of the deliveries came from George Dent, who made an oath before a justice of the peace in Baltimore County. He kept an account of the deliveries of James Johnson & Co. Thirty and one-quarter loads of bombshells, or 958 ten-inch shells, were shipped. The cost to the United States was £1,561, six pence, plus carriage of £7,562, ten shillings, one-fourth of which, or £1,890, twelve shillings, six pence, was to be paid to James Johnson & Co.[33]

Over three years later, the Johnsons were still trying to collect their account for the shells. In May 1784, Baker Johnson, on behalf of the four Johnson brothers, sent a memorial to the Congress of the United States:

> *Your memorialists...made a contract...for the casting of 10 Inch Bombshells...made and delivered at Baltimore Town...nine hundred and fifty eight Bombshells...that a considerable part of said shells were made use of at the seige of York[34] and the rest now remain in Baltimore Town...that your memorialists have rec'd a very small part of their money and were prevented from a settlement of their acct. by a pretended apprehension that the Shells remaining were faulty...your memorialists have procured some gentlemen of skill to prove the whole of said shells now in Baltimore amounting to 462—ten of which only appearing to be faulty—Your memoralists...apprehend upon every principle of justice they ought to be paid for the whole of the Shells which are good and applied to...the Commissioner for settling the accts. in Maryland to liquidate the claim...but...supposing that Mr. Hodgson, Commr. M. Stores, might have some evidence against the Soundness of Said Shells hath refused to settle and liquidate the Acct...unless especially authorized and directed by Congress...it may be determined whether the bombshells are good by a trial of them on the spot...Your memoralists pray...may receive either money or a certificate for the Balance due them.[35]*

The matter was referred to a committee of the Continental Congress on Monday, May 24, 1784. The committee collected copies of documents relating to the account, including David Poe's certification that he had 462 ten-inch bombshells, the remaining part of the shipment from James Johnson & Co. He said these shells had never been out of his possession and that he had not attempted to prove them until requested to do so on May 14 by Baker Johnson.[36]

When the committee of the Continental Congress contacted Daniel Joy, who had originally contracted with the Johnsons, it received the following reply:

Philadelphia, 2 June 1784
This is to certify whom it may concern that I proved a number of Bomb
Shells at Baltimore which were made by Messrs. James Johnson & Co.
of the State of Maryland, and found amongst them four hundred and
eighty two bad shells, they not being Air tight chiefly owing to a defect in
the ear of said Shells, they not being made any ways similar to the plan
& direction I left with the said Gentlemen when I contracted with them for
making Shells—If I had staid with them a few days, all would have been
well & their shells good, but the late Governor who was there repeatedly
declared to me that he had not a doubt but that his brother James would get
them executed in the best manner & agreeable to my direction, and as I was
then on my return & met with no Success Southward, & being anxious to
enlarge my Contracts with those whom I had the greatest expectations from.
I did not press myself to stay. If they had expressed the least desire of my
staying a few days I should not hesitated a moment to have complied.
[Signed] *Daniel Joy*[37]

James Hodgson, commissioner of military stores, gave additional information in his letter to the committee, dated June 3, 1784. Hodgson stated that the admission of Baker Johnson's claim "would have been injurious to the States." Captain Daniel Joy proved and condemned the shells while he and Mr. Hodgson were together. The reason for the condemnation was "their being cast without Staples or Ears in them altho' they were perforated for the purpose and the holes in which they should have been inserted were left open." Hodgson also stated that in an earlier return, Mr. Poe had noted that 482 of Mr. Johnson's shells were unfit for service. Hodgson said that he was always

disposed to make every proper allowance for a first attempt as was the
casting shells at Mr. Johnson's Furnace, but seeing as I did the faultiness
of the shells and knowing no remedy could be applied, I could not in justice
to the public admit them in his account.

This information had been communicated to Johnson's agent.[38] Mr. Hodgson enclosed a final accounting, including interest. The United States still owed James Johnson & Co. £435, eight shillings at the current rate of exchange for the 476 shells it had accepted.[39] The carriage was figured at a greatly reduced rate, and £445, eight shillings, one pence had already been paid to the Johnsons.

A question of the mode of proof was still being raised in December 1785. Secretary of War Henry Knox wrote to John White, commissioner of accounts for the State of Maryland, that he was trying to find out just what manner of proof was used on the shells.[40] The congressional committee had accepted the earlier recommendation of Captain Joy and James Hodgson, and their findings and accounting became part of the papers of the Continental Congress. The report of shot and shells made at a number of different furnaces and dated August 11, 1781, lists the 958 ten-inch shells made at Catoctin as the only munitions cast at the Frederick County furnace.[41]

As James Johnson & Co. continued operation, the village of Catoctin grew around the furnace complex. Houses for workmen were built, some of stone and some of logs. A large two-story stone ironmaster's house was built facing the furnace and casting house, providing a commanding view of the daily operations.[42] James Johnson probably never lived in this house if, as his son wrote, he lived on Auburn property until he moved into Springfield[43] in 1793.[44]

Catoctin was part of an extensive and closely connected system of iron operations that extended from Pennsylvania to Virginia. Workmen migrated about depending on the availability of work. One of these men, an ironmaster, John Rawlings, had come to Catoctin from Virginia to work with James Johnson. He had left "six head of Horned Cattle" in Virginia, and in November 1788, he sold them, "if they be not sold," and the balance of his possessions to the four Johnson brothers for £110, four shillings and eleven pence. His goods consisted of Prince, a five-year-old black gelding fifteen hands high, four featherbeds and bedsteads, two chests, six chairs and other articles of household furniture. Four Negro slaves who apparently had ironworking experience were included in the sale.[45] Rawlings was a migratory member of the ironworking community. His slaves were among the earliest blacks who were purchased to work at Catoctin Furnace.[46]

Over the years, each of the Johnson brothers had acquired extensive holdings, which were spread over Frederick County and into neighboring states. As the eighteenth century drew to a close, a number of land transfers were made among family members. Catoctin Furnace, rebuilt in 1787,[47] was operated by James Johnson & Co. until 1793. James Johnson also owned a forge, blacksmith shop, dwelling and other buildings on an 800-acre tract on Bush Creek.[48] He had built a large mansion house, Springfield, on his 1,030-acre manor near Catoctin and lived there from 1793 until his death in 1809.[49] Roger Johnson transferred his operation to Johnson Furnace and Bloomsbury Forge on the lower Monocacy, where he lived the balance of his life.

Thomas Johnson became more involved in the Patowmack[50] (Potomac) Company, a corporation set up to develop navigation on the Potomac River. He was also active in acquiring land for the District of Columbia. These interests drew his attention away from Catoctin, and he slowly liquidated his holdings in the area.

Thomas Johnson's interest in Potomac navigation led to an interesting encounter with James Rumsey, superintendent of the Potomac Company. Rumsey's job was to direct the building of canals around parts of the river that were not navigable. As he dealt with a steady stream of problems in his work, Rumsey gave thought to a project for navigation by steam. In the fall of 1785, Rumsey and his brother-in-law, Joseph Barnes, began to assemble a boat in Bath,[51] later moving it to Shepherdstown. Barnes contacted suppliers

Springfield, circa 1790, home of James Johnson, partner and ironmaster of Catoctin Furnace. *Photograph from the Historic American Building Survey, September 1936, in the collection of the Library of Congress.*

in Baltimore, Antietam and Catoctin for machinery parts. Thomas Johnson had James Johnson & Co. attempt to cast cylinders, but it was not successful in making them. Later, the cylinders were made of copper in Frederick Town.[52] Johnson was very supportive of Rumsey's experiment because, in his words,

> *if you can simplify the steam engine, render it cheap, and apply its powers to raise water in great quantities, for the purpose of agriculture and water works of all kinds…as has been much the subject of conversation between us at times, every man may easily perceive a vast field of improvement will thereby be opened.*[53]

Thomas and Baker Johnson operated the furnace as partners from 1793 to 1803, with Thomas holding a two-thirds interest and Baker one-third.[54] During this time, even though there were numerous land transfers, Thomas's interest in the furnace was evident because he was granted one-fourth of the iron ore on the parts of the Mountain Tract that George Calvert and John Davidson had bought. Thomas was also given "full and free liberty to dig, search for, raise, take and carry the same away."[55] The 1798 assessment listed Thomas and Baker Johnson as partners, owning Good Will and Stoney Park, 250 acres; the furnace; and a mill that was "altogether destroyed." The total value was £250.[56]

By 1803, Baker Johnson had increased his holdings at Catoctin until he not only owned the furnace[57] and adjoining lands but also had put together an impressive manor that joined James's Springfield. Baker named his 934-acre tract Auburn.[58] As he bought and expanded, Baker Johnson was developing a semi-feudal community common to ironworking operations.[59]

At the turn of the century, the furnace was leased to Benjamin Blackford and Thomas Thornburgh. Blackford was born in New Jersey in October 1767, at the time the crisis between the colonies and the mother country was sharpening, and as a mere lad he had served at Yorktown, where he witnessed the British surrender. After the Revolution, Blackford found employment as a clerk for Eugene Thornburgh, a friend of his father, at Pine Grove Furnace.[60] The Thornburghs had operated Pine Grove Furnace and Thornburgh Forge in Cumberland County, Pennsylvania, since the mid-1760s.[61] Thomas Thornburgh and young Blackford went into partnership. Their venture must have been very successful. According to family tradition, by the time Blackford was twenty-one years old he had accumulated $1,000 for every year of his life. He married Isabella Arthur of Carlisle, Pennsylvania, and they had several children while still at Pine Grove. One of the children was named for Thomas Thornburgh. After Blackford leased Catoctin Furnace, the family moved to Maryland. During their stay at Catoctin, three more children were born, in August 1801, February 1804 and October 1806.[62] The Blackfords probably lived in the ironmaster's residence that had been built during the proprietorship of James Johnson. The furnace continued production of household and industrial items, including Catoctin stoves and fire backs.

Left: Portrait of Benjamin Blackford, operator of Catoctin Furnace, 1801–11. *Photograph from the Blackford Family History held by the Historical Society of Frederick County, Inc.*

Below: Blackford and Thornburgh fire back, circa 1801–11, from the dining room of Auburn. *Photograph courtesy of Mr. and Mrs. C.E. Gardiner.*

Auburn, a Georgian, three-story stone manor house constructed by Baker Johnson circa 1805, as it appears today. *Photography courtesy of Donald Frame.*

During the years that the furnace was leased to Blackford, Baker Johnson began construction of a mansion house on the Auburn tract and completed it about 1805. It is not certain how long he lived at Auburn because, when he wrote his will on February 22, 1809, he divided the Auburn lands, leaving Baker Jr. "that part of my lands where he now lives which has been resurveyed by the name of 'Auburn' [and] "all the household Furniture at Auburn."[63] His will further stated that his wife, Catherine, was to get "the use of the house and lots where we now live with the use of the whole of the furniture." The location of the "house and lots where we now live" was further defined in his division to his sons Worthington and Charles after Catherine Johnson's death. "The house and part of the lots where we now live…to be divided…from Market Street to run with the brick wall under the woodhouse." The Johnsons were living in Frederick, and Baker Jr. was living at Auburn.

Baker Johnson Sr., who was described as a "most hospitable and kind friend…whose house was proverbial for unbounded hospitality,"[64] had a highly successful law practice in Frederick, Montgomery and Washington Counties. When he divided his extensive properties among his wife and children in his 1809 will, he directed that the

Auburn, the Baker Johnson Sr. farmstead, circa 1900, looking across the pond later removed during construction of U.S. 15. *Photograph courtesy of Mr. and Mrs. C.E. Gardiner.*

Catoctin Furnace and all the lands annexed and appropriated to it...I wish sold to Mr. Blackford and which I estimate at twelve thousand pounds. I look on him a good man. I ever have been and still am his sincere friend and hope and expect he will esteem the terms just and reasonable.[65]

However, in a codicil dated March 7, 1811, Johnson directed his executors to

sell on such terms and in such manner as to them shall seem and appear... most beneficial...the money...from the sale of the said furnace and lands shall be equally divided among my four daughters.[66]

Johnson died on June 18, 1811, and when the property was advertised for public sale, the listing included

a large blast furnace—the stack wheel and bellows and all the buildings of the furnace are built in the best manner and are in complete order... land attached thereto (all adjoining each other)...4,611 acres 600– 700 acres...arable, 60 acres meadow (well set with timothy)...residue of land is well covered with wood and young timber, and is deemed sufficient to furnish coal wood...for many years...ore immediately on the spot...superior quality...apparently inexhaustible. Stream is constant... limestone quarry...very convenient, not more than 200 yards from the furnace bank. Other improvements...consist of a large two story stone dwelling house with necessary out-houses...and a fountain pump at the kitchen door. Two convenient store houses, a chopping mill, stone smith shop, barns, stables, corn houses, also from 15 to 20 houses for the accommodation of workmen.[67]

Blackford must have already indicated his plans to locate elsewhere because the advertisement also said that the "lease will expire on first of April [1812] and he will show the premises to any person inclined to purchase the same and give...immediate privilege...of doing all things necessary to prepare for a blast."[68] The Blackfords left Catoctin at the expiration of the lease and bought a tract in Page County, Virginia, where they operated the Isabella Furnace.

Catoctin Furnace was now an established business. It had survived the Revolution. It was ready to take its place as a producer in the young republic.

Artist's rendition of Catoctin Furnace Village in the early nineteenth century, by local artist Kris Smith. *Courtesy of Catoctin Furnace Historical Society.*

Chapter 2

THE MIDDLE YEARS

During the next half century of operation, the ironworking business at Catoctin alternately flourished and failed. It was expanded and improved, but national financial crises greatly affected the possibility of profit. The product, as well as the mode of operation, reflected the changing times. There was a shift from stove and hardware casting to the production of pig iron.

Word that Catoctin Furnace was being offered for sale was spread by newspaper advertisement and attracted the attention of the Mayberry family, ironmasters from the Philadelphia area. The Mayberrys had owned and operated several furnaces and forges, among them Mount Holly in Burlington County, New Jersey. In the early days of the Revolution, Mount Holly had been engaged in making shot, shells and kettles for the Continental army. When the British learned that munitions of war were being made at the furnace, they destroyed it. Thomas Mayberry did not rebuild at Mount Holly.[69]

On November 3, 1785, Thomas Mayberry was a signer of a petition to the General Assembly of Pennsylvania asking protection for the iron industry and recommending duties on foreign bar iron to help hold down imports.[70] Duties imposed by Congress near the end of the century had the effect of raising the price of imported iron. In spite of this, improved machinery and production methods in Europe pushed their exports to a new high and seriously threatened the domestic iron industry.

Iron manufacture was an expensive and risky business to maintain. Wood had to be cut, made into charcoal and hauled to the furnace. The ore had to be dug and transported. Production was dependent not only on the skill of the workers but also on the vagaries of the weather. Water powered the wheel that ran the furnace bellows. A dry season meant weak or irregular power. At times, the operation had to shut down completely.

On August 15, 1811, Willoughby Mayberry and Thomas Mayberry bought the Catoctin Furnace from the executors of Baker Johnson for £12,500 current money.[71] The partnership was short lived, for on March 9, 1813, Willoughby bought out Thomas for $20,000 and became sole owner.[72] In June 1812, war had broken out between the United States and Britain. Willoughby Mayberry used the wartime prosperity to make improvements to his property. He built some new houses for workmen and a second blacksmith shop and began construction of a two-story stone house on one of the farms attached to the property.[73]

Duties on imports were increased 100 percent. Demand for iron production in the States was enormous. It seemed that Catoctin would flourish under Mayberry ownership, but the wartime boom collapsed. In 1814, government policy shifted to free trade. Many iron operations were ruined, Catoctin among them. Unable to meet his obligations, Willoughby Mayberry borrowed $8,000 from Jeremiah Mayberry of Northern Liberties, a township in Philadelphia County, Pennsylvania, using the furnace property as collateral.[74] In late October 1819, the Mayberry operation went bankrupt. All the horses, harnesses, wagons and tools used in the furnace business, as well as Mayberry's own cows, hogs, household furniture, dishes

Vallonne manor house, circa 1815, believed to be associated with the Mayberry family. The current name is Windy Hill Farm. *Photograph courtesy of Donald Frame.*

A Franklin stove in the Waesche house, Thurmont, Maryland, produced by John Brien. Brien operated Catoctin Furnace from 1820 to 1834. *Photograph courtesy of Joel T. Anderson.*

and silverware, were sold for $4,000 to Jeremiah Mayberry.[75] Willoughby Mayberry moved with his family to Jefferson County, Virginia,[76] to start over operating Vestal Furnace. On May 2, 1820, Catoctin was put up for sale by the sheriff of Frederick County.[77] John Brien bought the property for $27,505.[78] Brien was the son-in-law of Colonel John McPherson, who had extensive landholdings and industrial interests in western Maryland. Among the enterprises in which McPherson and Brien were involved was Antietam Furnace in Washington County. John Brien also had other ties to the iron industry. His brother-in-law, John McPherson Jr., married Frances Johnson, granddaughter of Thomas Johnson. Also, Brien had close ties with Robert and William Coleman of Cornwall Furnace in Pennsylvania. He named two of his sons Robert Coleman Brien and William Coleman Brien.

The 1820 census of manufactures listed Brien at Catoctin Furnace, lately purchased, with $60,000 capital, eighty hands, one wheel, two cylinder bellows, a small chopping mill out of order and a sawmill for his own use. The works was closed, undergoing repairs, and last used as a casting furnace, "an old establishment out of repair." Brien produced six to nine hundred tons per year to make holloware and the cast-iron Catoctin stove.

Detail of a John Brien Franklin stove. *Photograph courtesy of Joel T. Anderson.*

A ten-plate cast-iron stove produced by John Brien at Catoctin Furnace. Brien operated the furnace from 1820 to 1834. An identical stove is on display at the Cunningham Falls State Park Visitors' Center, courtesy of the Catoctin Furnace Historical Society. *Photograph courtesy of the Henry Francis du Pont Winterthur Museum.*

Portrait of an Iron-Making Village

During his ownership of Catoctin Furnace, John Brien added extensively to the property holdings. He bought additional mountain land and brought the manors that had been developed by the Johnsons back into Catoctin ownership. Auburn was sold to Brien at a sheriff's sale on April 11, 1826, for $10,000.[79] In 1831, John Brien rebuilt the furnace, enlarging it to a height of thirty-three feet and to an interior width of nine feet.[80] Building stones, which were noted for their fire resistance, were found near the mouth of the Monocacy River. These stones were used in the furnace and lime kilns close by, including Catoctin. Pig iron was hauled by horse-drawn wagons to Frederick for shipment, and on the return, materials such as building stone were hauled back to Catoctin, a two-day round trip.[81] A gristmill was added to the complex, and Brien enlarged and improved the ironmaster's house, bringing it more into keeping with its position as executive and social center of the iron plantation.[82] Brien was a very public-spirited citizen, for he built a small chapel and likely provided some sort of school facility during the years he owned the furnace complex.[83]

The front façade of the Catoctin Furnace ironmaster's house. Constructed early in the furnace's history, John Brien substantially enlarged and improved the structure. *Photograph courtesy of the collection of Mary Rae Cantwell.*

The rear elevation of the ironmaster's mansion (Catoctin House) showing buttresses supporting the wall. *Photograph from the Historic American Building Survey, September 1936, in the collection of the Library of Congress.*

Death brought rapid and devastating changes to the operation of Catoctin under John Brien. At the time he bought the furnace, the Brien family consisted of John and Harriet (McPherson); their sons, Robert Coleman, John McPherson, Henry Augustus, Edward and William Coleman; and a daughter, Harriet S(mith). In 1827, Harriet McPherson Brien died, followed in 1829 by her father, John McPherson. The iron-making interests of McPherson were willed to his son Horatio, who sold them to John McPherson Brien in the estate settlement.[84] For a short time, Brien father and son had common business interests in Antietam and Catoctin.

The year 1834 brought the death of Robert Coleman Brien, followed by the death of his father, John, and his brother William. The devastation caused by these deaths was heightened because there were no wills to guide the disposition of the property. John McPherson Jr. was appointed trustee to settle the estate. Legal battles dragged on for years as Katherine Hughes Brien, widow of William and granddaughter of Daniel Hughes, one of the early operators of Antietam Furnace, tried to gain her dower right to her deceased husband's share of the Brien estate.[85] This was finally settled for $6,000.[86]

Even though John Brien had extensive property, he had also become deeply indebted. His court-appointed trustee, John McPherson Jr., sold some holdings over the next several years and partially settled the debts.[87] John McPherson Brien continued to operate a nail works in Antietam, while Henry A. Brien ran Catoctin Furnace. In a letter to his uncle John McPherson Jr., dated February 2, 1835, Henry sent $100 for new hearth stones for the furnace.[88]

In December 1841, John McPherson Brien bought Catoctin Furnace from his father's estate for $20,315.[89] John McPherson, trustee, advertised "Catoctin Iron Works" in the *Baltimore American* on November 22, 1841, prior to the December 22 auction. The complex included some 7,500 acres of timberland, along with ore "of superior quality." Output was eight to nine hundred tons of pig iron per annum; the associated merchant mill with two pairs of burrs and a daily maximum capacity of forty barrels. The sawmill was first rate, nearly new. McPherson noted:

> *The castings have always been distinguished for their smoothness, neatness and durability. There is a sufficient number of stone and log dwelling houses for all necessary hands, also a superior Dwelling house, Stables, Carriage House, large and handsome garden, an ice house, a store house and all necessary out houses for the accommodation of the owner if he should wish to reside there.*

Brien, who had debts in excess of $100,000 secured by Robert Gilmor of Baltimore, gave Gilmor a mortgage on the Catoctin Furnace and Ironworks, Antietam Ironworks, fifty-four slaves, six mule teams and three horse teams, along with wagons and gear.[90] His financial condition did not improve, for six months later the mortgage was expanded to include a two-thirds interest in the 550-acre Auburn tract, as well as "ten thousand cords of wood, thirty thousand bushels of stove coal, twenty-five thousand pounds of bacon, four hundred kegs of nails…three hundred tons of Pig Iron, fifty tons Bar Iron, fifty tons Bloom."[91]

The credit restrictions of the early 1830s were lifted at about the same time the Brien brothers took over their late father's business interests. An inflationary boom followed, reflected in the 1836 export value of $29.95 a ton for pig iron. There was wild speculation in land, slaves and domestic improvements. As the Andrew Jackson administration moved to stop land speculation, inflated prices plummeted. By 1841, the export value of pig iron per ton was just $15.80.[92] A firm with the heavy debt load carried by the Briens could not compete, in spite of the fact that they were apparently innovative businessmen. As early as 1836, Henry A. Brien and Co. was using the newly opened Baltimore and Ohio Railroad to ship castings to Henry Thompson & Son, merchants in Baltimore.[93]

Less than two years after he bought the Catoctin Furnace complex, John McPherson Brien was forced to sell it. On April 22, 1843, he gave a contract to Peregrine Fitzhugh. Fitzhugh was a descendant of a planter family of Virginia. His grandfather, Colonel Peregrine Fitzhugh, was an officer in the Revolutionary army and married Elizabeth Chew of Washington County, Maryland.[94] There were family ties to ironworking interests, because Colonel Fitzhugh's brother William, who also was a Revolutionary army officer, married Ann Hughes, daughter of Daniel Hughes of the Antietam and Cecil Furnaces. There was much intermarriage among the Hughes, McPherson and Fitzhugh families, all of whom had interests in early industrialization. Peregrine Fitzhugh's great-aunt Henrietta Chew Galloway was the widow of Benjamin Galloway, a prominent Washington County politician.[95] At her death in 1847, her estate was left to her three great-nephews, and Peregrine was now financially able to improve his Catoctin Furnace property. Fitzhugh marketed much of his pig iron through commission merchants. The rapidly developing railroad system demanded large amounts of iron, and some of Catoctin's production was sold to the Lobdell Car Wheel Works of Wilmington, Delaware.[96]

In an effort to increase the efficiency of his operation, Fitzhugh entered into an agreement with Michael M. Ege about 1849. Ege had an interesting and impressive background in iron making. He was a descendant of George Michael and Anna Catherine (Holz) Ege. When George Michael Ege died about 1758, his wife and two small sons, George and Michael, were taken into the home of her sister, Elizabeth Holz Stiegel, and her husband, Henry William Stiegel. At that time, Stiegel was operating Elizabeth Furnace in eastern Pennsylvania. He treated the Ege children like his own sons, teaching them the business so that they became very prominent among Pennsylvania ironmasters. Stiegel later operated the glassmaking business that brought him renown. George Ege was at one time part owner of Cornwall Furnace with Robert Coleman, the uncle of John Brien.[97] Bringing his expertise to Catoctin, Michael Ege, a later generation ironmaster, remained in business with Fitzhugh until September 1853. At the time he left, the works were said to be in good repair and in regular blast, doing a better business than at any time for some years past.[98]

The improved financial situation did not last long. Fitzhugh had persistent financial stresses. He borrowed money using his mother and wife, who had independent resources, as surety. He sold land, including Auburn in 1855, but stipulated that the purchasers, the McPherson family, could not mine ore or build a furnace on it.[99] Even the weather caused problems for Peregrine Fitzhugh. The summer of 1854 brought a disastrous drought to the county. Streams dried up so that there was not enough water to turn the wheel powering the bellows. Production was at a minimum, and very little ore was shipped.[100]

In November 1856, Fitzhugh entered into a co-partnership with Jacob M. Kunkel of Frederick as a means of raising money. Kunkel paid $35,000 for his share of the seven-thousand-acre property and for tools, wagons, carts, ore, charcoal, horses, mules and furnace and railroad cars.[101] Fitzhugh used the money realized from this and other financing schemes to improve the property. He was responsible for installing the rails and cars that brought ore from the ore bank to the furnace. Fitzhugh also built a second furnace alongside the original stack. This new stack, erected in 1857, was a steam-powered hot-blast charcoal furnace and was given the name Isabella. It was the same size and was built to operate with the same ore as the original furnace.[102]

Peregrine Fitzhugh was another ironmaster with great civic interests. In 1855, because of his interest in the revitalization of Harriet Chapel, he deeded to the Episcopal Diocese of Maryland seven acres of land surrounding the little chapel built by John Brien.[103] Fitzhugh also provided

Isabella stack, constructed in 1857 during the Fitzhugh-Jacob Kunkel partnership. *Photograph from the Historic American Building Survey, September 1936, in the collection of the Library of Congress.*

The Catoctin Parish Rectory, 1855–1907, donated to the parish by Peregrine and Sara Margaret Fitzhugh on April 14, 1855. *Photograph courtesy of the Diocese of Maryland.*

a sort of medical plan for his employees. In 1849, the young Dr. William S. McPherson Jr., who had family ties to Catoctin and to the Fitzhugh family, moved into Auburn and provided the workmen with some medical services. He made an agreement with Fitzhugh in January 1855 to be paid $600 per annum for the practice at the furnace operations and for the Fitzhugh family.[104]

The severe national economic decline in 1857 put an extra burden on the operation at Catoctin. It was a bad time for Jacob Kunkel to have invested in an iron furnace. Catoctin was in one of its financial valleys, but there were exciting and productive days ahead.

Chapter 3

SUMMIT AND DECLINE

The years between 1856 and 1912 witnessed the greatest productivity of Catoctin Furnace, followed by uncertainty and, finally, a complete shutdown. Changing technology caught up with the industry that had furnished jobs for so many. As its life had a profound effect on the area, the effect of its death was also traumatic.

The involvement of the Kunkel family in the iron industry at Catoctin Furnace introduced a new dimension to the operation of the business. Jacob Kunkel, a prominent attorney, state senator and member of Congress,[105] was not directly involved in managing. He left these duties in the hands of Peregrine Fitzhugh. Their agreement stated that Fitzhugh was to give his "sole and exclusive attention" to the business. In turn, he could occupy the mansion house and would be provided firewood for his family; stabling and pasture for his horses, cows and hogs; and the privilege of buying at "first cost" any goods and groceries his family used from the company store.[106] Neither partner could take more than $1,500 quarterly from the business, which would be deducted from his share of the profits. Kunkel was to pay a manager to help out in his place. Both men shared control, and Kunkel did take note of the operation of the business. He was not pleased with Fitzhugh's handling of it, and less than two years after the partnership was set up, he asked for its dissolution. On April 21, 1858, the partners executed an agreement to separate, with Fitzhugh continuing to operate the business in order to apply the net profit to partnership debts. Kunkel held a mortgage on the property.[107]

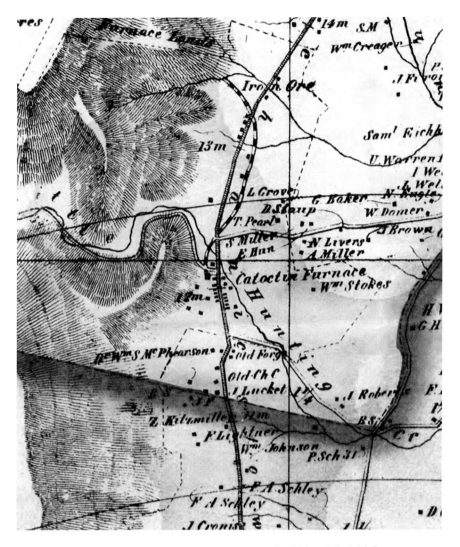

The Catoctin Furnace complex and village on the *Isaac Bond Map of Frederick County, Maryland*, 1858. *Map on file with the Map and Geography Reading Room of the Library of Congress.*

In October 1858, suit was brought against Fitzhugh by several of his debtors, and the court appointed William Ross and John Baker Kunkel, brother of Jacob, as trustees of the property.[108] On December 15, 1858, John Kunkel, father of Jacob M. and John Baker Kunkel, bought the property for $51,000.[109] John Kunkel was a Frederick tanner and a very successful businessman. He was then seventy-seven years old and bought the iron business as an investment. Within a few months of the purchase, his son, John Baker, moved into the ironmaster's house and began operation.

A trustee's sale advertised Catoctin Furnace and Ironworks, saw- and gristmill, sixty houses, etc., two furnaces each, with a vertical direct action blowing engine built by J.P. Morris of Philadelphia.[110]

Following the sale of his property, Peregrine Fitzhugh left Catoctin to travel to Texas. His family remained in the ironmaster's house, and records of the business were left in a drawer of Fitzhugh's private desk. His wife had to leave when Kunkel moved into the mansion, so she took her family and personal possessions to Auburn until her husband returned in the spring of 1859. The family later returned to Texas and eventually went to California.[111]

The 1860 census of manufacturers listed J.B. Kunkel and brother as owners of Catoctin Furnace, with $100,000 capital investment, ninety employees and an eighty-horsepower steam engine. Annual output was 4,500 tons of pig iron ($100,000) made from 12,000 tons of ore.

John Kunkel died in 1861 after having paid only one of the notes given at the time of purchase. He still owed $28,687.50 in notes not yet due and had never received a deed to the property.[112] According to the terms of his will, John Kunkel left the property to his two sons. Jacob was involved with his law practice, so in 1866 he sold his half of the iron-making business to his brother for $60,000.[113]

Under John Baker Kunkel's management, the Catoctin Ironworks grew to its greatest scope and production. Kunkel bought extensive property to add to the 7,000 acres in the original purchase. At its largest extent, there were 11,350 acres of land in the complex, involving both farmland and mountain tracts.[114] In 1873, Kunkel also built a third furnace, which he named Deborah after his wife. This stack, a coke furnace, was built as an iron, brick-lined cylinder fifty feet high and eleven and a half feet inside diameter.[115] Deborah had an annual capacity of 9,000 tons, specifically described as a 35-ton-per-diem or 1,200-per-annum output of car wheel iron.[116] The product was shipped to foundries and marketed through commission merchants for such fabricators as Lobdell Car Wheel Company. Because of the middleman involved in buying pig iron from suppliers and routing it for foundry and milling processes, it is virtually impossible to verify the story about Catoctin iron being used to make plates for the *Monitor.*

The economic condition of the enterprise was sound, as demonstrated in the 1867 *Bradstreet Directory* that listed J.B. Kunkel & Bros., iron manufacturers "and variety store" with a BC credit rating (good credit).

Portrait of an Iron-Making Village

The Deborah stack with stock house on the right and Monocacy Valley Railroad tracks coming into the complex. A possible Dinky railroad trestle can be seen in front of the stock house. Note the deforested mountain in the background. *Photo courtesy of the Catoctin Furnace Historical Society.*

The Deborah stack, boiler house and casting shed in the foreground. The stock house is in the upper left background. *Photo courtesy of the Catoctin Furnace Historical Society.*

In 1876, John B. Kunkel applied for a patent for an improved iron-making process that eliminated phosphorus from iron by means of magnesian limestone, a double carbonate of lime and magnesia.[117] Operation of the furnace did not seem to change significantly after the patent was applied for. The major change came about as a result of putting up the Deborah stack, which increased production about 600 percent over the older charcoal furnace. The tax records for 1876 list three furnaces.[118] However, the Johnson cold-blast furnace was shut down by Kunkel.[119] He continued to use one charcoal furnace, keeping his mountain land for charcoaling.

At the height of his operation, Kunkel employed about five hundred men in the various operations, including mining; charcoaling; operation of the furnaces, sawmill, gristmill, store, farms and ore railroad; and property construction and maintenance.[120] He added significantly to the houses for workmen, owning about eighty.[121] Also, in November 1868, he gave the Frederick County Board of School Commissioners one acre of land about one-quarter of a mile north of the furnace.[122] The school built on this land served the furnace district for over sixty years.[123]

View looking north toward the furnace and ironmaster's house, showing the log and stone worker housing. *Photograph from the Historic American Building Survey, September 1936, in the collection of the Library of Congress.*

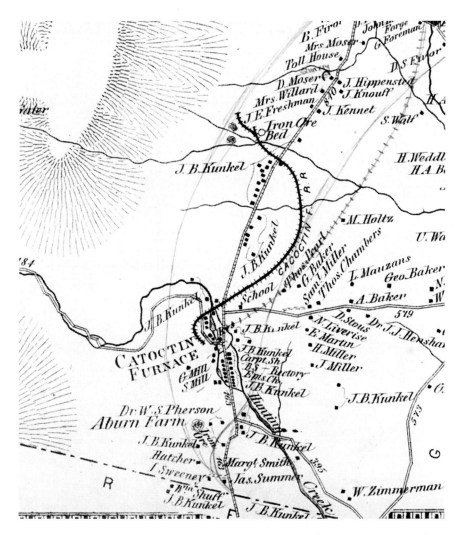

An 1873 *D.J. Lake Atlas of Frederick County, Maryland*, showing the Catoctin Furnace complex with the narrow-gage Dinky Railroad connecting the upper ore bank to the furnace complex. *Map on file with the Map and Geography Reading Room of the Library of Congress.*

John B. Kunkel died on April 5, 1885, at the age of sixty-eight, leaving no will.[124] His children conveyed their interests in the Catoctin iron furnace to a company they set up, naming it Catoctin Iron Company.[125] Within a few months, they sold about 688 acres of land in small tracts on the westernmost reaches of the holdings. L.R. Waesche, who had started work for Kunkel in 1882 as bookkeeper, became manager for them. This was the first time in the history of the furnace that there was not direct owner management in the operation. In 1886, Waesche and Steiner Schley built the Monocacy Valley Railroad from Catoctin Furnace to Thurmont, where it connected with the western Maryland, making receipt and shipment of products much faster and easier. The *Manufacturers Record* of May 7, 1887, reported, "The Catoctin Iron Co. have blown in another furnace." At this time, the furnace was producing about thirty tons of iron per day.[126]

In 1888, the Kunkel estate was sued by Pearre Brothers & Co., forcing its economic problems into the hands of the court. William P. Maulsby Jr. and Charles W. Ross were appointed as trustees and, on May 24, 1888, held a sale at the City Hotel in Frederick. The purchaser was Thomas Gorsuch of Westminster, who bought 10,677 acres of land, as well as the furnaces, ironmaster's mansion, mills, about eighty "tenement houses" and four lots in Frederick for $75,001.[127] The growing crops of grain on Windy Hill Farm were reserved for the tenant. Gorsuch was acting as agent for a group of investors who formed a corporate body, the Catoctin Mountain Iron Company, which operated the iron complex until 1892. Although the Catoctin Mountain Iron Company started a paint mill as a sideline, low iron prices and uncompetitive production costs forced the company to shut

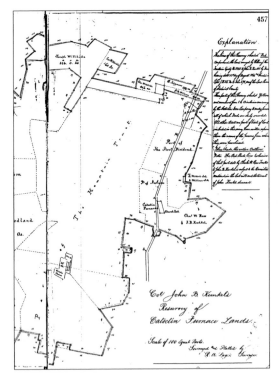

An 1888 plat of the Catoctin Furnace tract, from the Frederick County Equity Case 5229. *Archived in the Maryland State Archives.*

Portrait of an Iron-Making Village

Harry Peyton Gorsuch and friends at the Catoctin Furnace Bridge of the Dinky Railroad over Little Hunting Creek. *Photograph courtesy of the Maryland State Archives.*

Workers at Catoctin Furnace in full operation, circa 1890. Deborah, on the left, is in blast; Isabella, on the right, still retains the boiler and air heater but is not in operation. Stacks of pig iron are visible in the background right. *Photograph courtesy of the Catoctin Furnace Historical Society.*

down in 1892. The paint mill produced blue, red and yellow ochre from the clay banks north of the furnace.[128]

For most of the years from 1892 to 1898, the furnace sat idle. Nationally, it was a time of severe depression, labor unrest and business failures. The effect on the working population of Catoctin Furnace was devastating. It is no wonder that a hopeful *Frederick News* article from March 1899 stated:

> *It is understood that the paint works will be resumed and that a nail and hosiery industry will be established…giving employment to hundreds… extensive smelting plant will again be started up…many former residents of that vicinity have left for new fields of enterprise…still a large number of people residing in that section will welcome…that prospects are good for rekindling the fires which formerly made that place famous.*[129]

It was not to be. The court-appointed trustees, who had advertised the property after the death of Thomas Gorsuch in 1898, finally sold the complex to Ernest and Willa Sharp of Baltimore for $30,000, with $4,000 down and a $26,000 mortgage.[130] On August 1, 1899, the Sharps transferred the property to the Blue Mountain Iron and Steel Corporation of Baltimore for $580,000, a highly inflated figure for purposes of stock issue. The corporation planned to issue $500,000 worth of bonds to raise money to improve the property. The Sharps were paid in company stock and an agreement to pay off the mortgage on their original purchase.[131]

Repairs were started, and the mines reopened in October 1899.[132] By April 1900, the company was ready to go into production, and by enlarging the Deborah furnace, an output of forty tons per day was reached.[133] Financial troubles continued, and the property,

> *which has been tied up in a consequence of a series of legal complications, announced today, through their local attorneys, that they have made satisfactory arrangements to liquidate all indebtedness and will open the furnaces tomorrow in full blast.*[134]

The entire Catoctin Furnace operation was advertised for sale with a lengthy and detailed description in the *Sun* on January 22, 1902:

> *FIRST—The property known as The Catoctin Iron Works and the lands thereto attached situated on the Frederick and Emmitsburg Turnpike road, at the base of the Catoctin range of mountains, and about 12 miles from*

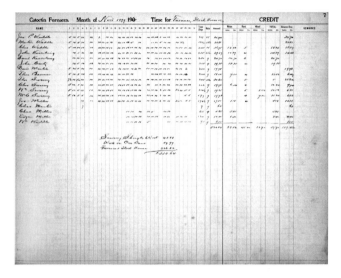

A page from the *Upper Mine Ledger,* dated November 1899. *Donated by William Green to the author, original now in the collection of the Historical Society of Frederick County, Inc. archives.*

Frederick City and about three miles south of Thurmont, a station on the Western Maryland Railroad; said Furnace property is connected with the railroad mentioned by a railroad known as Monocacy Valley Railroad. The land in this tract is about 7,000 acres, more or less. The improvements on the property are:

(a) A COKE FURNACE, *lately put in good condition throughout, and now engaged in making iron at the rate of about 25 tons per day, and with a capacity of between 40 and 50 tons.*

(b) A CHARCOAL FURNACE, *now divested of machinery.*

(c) A LARGE FRAME MILL, *with ample water power, formerly used for grinding, oxidizing and preparing ochers and umbers.*

(d) A large FRAME STORE AND OFFICE BUILDING.

(e) A large two-story well built and lately repaired 16-room DWELLING HOUSE, *with all necessary Outbuildings.*

(f) CARPENTER AND BLACKSMITH SHOPS, CARRIAGE, LUMBER, CORNHOUSE, STABLES FOR 30 HORSES, LARGE ICEHOUSE, ETC.

(G) About 65 TENEMENT HOUSES *for the use of the employees about and at the Furnace, and which are capable of yielding about $120 per month rent.*

The entire property has been repaired and put in good shape within the past 18 months and possesses all the accessories of a going business in a good condition. There are on this tract large deposits of hematite ore, which are readily accessible, and are believed to be practically inexhaustible. The ore is of excellent quality, in close proximity to the Furnace, and is now in use at the Furnace, the ore mines being furnished with washers, pumps, etc.

A deposit of magnetic iron ore of great richness has been traced for two miles upon the property; this deposit is undeveloped further than by a number of shallow shafts, but there is believed to be every indication of a very large and rich deposit of this ore. There are also believed to be on this tract large beds of ochers and umbers of rich shade and a superior quality, capable of being mined and prepared at a very low cost. There are also large quantities of pure white flint upon the property suitable for potteries.

This property offers a rare chance for capitalists and investors. With proper management and capital to operate and develop the many resources no better opportunity can be afforded for a profitable investment and business.

SECOND—A tract of about 3,000 ACRES OF MOUNTAIN LAND lying west of tract No. 1 and adjoining the same; this tract is largely covered with timber—Chestnut, Locust, Poplar, etc.

Tracts Nos. 1 and 2 will be offered together or separately, as may be deemed best by the undersigned on the day of the sale.

The advertisement for sale included dwellings, lots and warehouses in Frederick City, and all were to be sold as part of this assignee-mortgagee's public sale.

Blue Mountain Iron and Steel Corporation remained in operation until February 1903, when the furnace fires were extinguished for the last

Upper Ore Bank, circa 1900, using a Vulcan steam shovel. Photo annotations by William Renner, longtime resident and Catoctin Furnace employee. *Photograph courtesy of the Catoctin Furnace Historical Society.*

Workers apparently dismantling the Deborah stack for transport to Bedford, Pennsylvania, during Joseph Thropp's ownership. *Photograph by the O'Toole Studio of Thurmont, Maryland, courtesy of the Thurmont Historical Society.*

time.[135] After being adjudged bankrupt, the property was sold again at public auction, this time in February 1906, to Joseph E. Thropp, a large independent iron operator and owner of Earlston furnaces in Bedford County, Pennsylvania.[136] The purchase price was $44,950.50 for the real property and $6,185 for the machinery and equipment, a total of $51,135.[137] Thropp, a former member of Congress from Bedford, was expected to develop the property and make it flourish again. Instead, he dismantled the furnace, taking everything that was usable to his Pennsylvania operation. He worked the mines until 1912, shipping the ore to his Everett furnaces.

The shutdown of the Catoctin iron complex marked the end of an era. It had survived for nearly a century and a half. The ore from Catoctin Mountain had been used for products for home and farm. Some of the products had a peaceful use; others were tools of war. Some stayed close by; others were used far from Catoctin. All contributed to the growth and development of this nation.

Chapter 4

A TECHNICAL HISTORY OF CATOCTIN FURNACE

By Joel T. Anderson

T he Catoctin iron furnace operated almost continuously from 1776 to 1903. During this period, both charcoal and coke from bituminous coal were used as fuel for the furnace. The products of this furnace were both raw pig iron and holloware such as stoves, kitchen utensils and tools. This chapter will discuss how the furnace operated, materials needed in the operation, the final products and the eventual shutdown.[138]

In the years preceding the American War of Independence, the forests of Britain and Europe were greatly depleted due to the high demand for charcoal for iron manufacturing. The depletion of these forests caused Britain and the nations of southern and central Europe to import iron manufactured in countries on the fringes of Europe, such as Russia and areas in Scandinavia. This practice caused Britain to lose hard currency in the trade, and this, under the prevailing economic theory of mercantilism, was considered very bad for the British economy.

While the resources of the British mainland that were required for iron manufacturing were being depleted, relatively large deposits of iron ore were being discovered on the eastern seaboard of North America. The existence of these ores and the availability of massive amounts of timber and adequate water made the manufacture of iron there very desirable.

The mercantilist system made it much more desirable for Britain to import iron from its North American colonies than to buy it from its neighbors on the European continent. If Britain received its iron from its colonies, it usually paid for it with finished products rather than having to give up hard currency. It is important to note that the British Parliament passed numerous laws with the intention of allowing the colonies to manufacture only wrought iron. All refining and forging, the British believed, should be done in Britain. This would ensure that the British were not buying what they believed to be finished products. They were buying what they considered to be a raw material—pig iron—which they could refine and use or sell back to the colonies in order to pay for the original iron.

It was in this environment that the Johnson brothers set out in 1774 to build an iron furnace. Significant iron ore deposits of good quality had been discovered along the base of the mountain in the area near present-day Catoctin Furnace. This, along with adequate amounts of timber and a good stream, made an excellent location to construct an iron furnace.

In the summer of 1776, the original Catoctin Furnace stack was put into blast, probably next to where the existing furnace stands. However, one early source indicates that it was moved to this site from farther downstream in 1787, when the stack was rebuilt.[139] This original furnace was a cold-blast, water-powered operation. At this time, the North American iron industry was exclusively using cold blast technology, although it was during this period that the British were beginning to look at technical improvements such as hot blast to improve efficiency.

The blast in an iron furnace such as Catoctin Furnace is the injection of air through a device called a *tuyere* at the base of the furnace. The blast

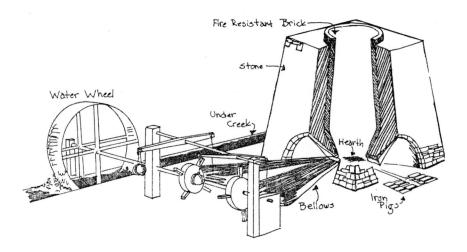

Diagram of a cold-blast charcoal iron furnace. *Courtesy of Cunningham Falls State Park.*

Casting arch at the base of the Isabella stack. This photograph is believed to date to circa 1936 and the federal acquisition of the furnace. *Photograph courtesy of the Catoctin Furnace Historical Society.*

is the source of oxygen required for the charcoal to burn. Up through the latter half of the eighteenth century, blast was usually provided by a very large bellows being operated up and down by a crankshaft type of device, which in turn was connected to a water wheel. This was the case at Catoctin Furnace, where Little Hunting Creek was the source of water for power.

An extensive water race and other facilities, along with a location where a significant drop existed in the creek or water source, were necessary to carry the water from the creek bed over the top of the water wheel to provide power. At Catoctin Furnace, water was diverted from Little Hunting Creek, several hundred yards from the furnace location. A series of dams was built to catch the water and hold it in preparation for its trip down the raceway. After the water had gone over the water wheel, driving the bellows, it followed a raceway down through the village of Catoctin Furnace, which lies to the south of the furnace stack. By the time the water reached the stack, the water was already several hundred feet to the south of Little Hunting Creek, and as it moved down through the village to the end of the raceway, at one point it was over a quarter of a mile to the southwest of the creek. The raceway apparently followed this course for at least two reasons. One reason was to achieve sufficient drop in order to reunite with the water source. This was a significant problem because the base of the furnace site actually is situated lower than Little Hunting Creek at its closest point to the furnace stack. The second reason was to provide an opportunity for the water to be reused farther down the raceway to operate other small enterprises. It is important to note that in the beginning of its use, the raceway was likely not built with this in mind, since these enterprises did not come until later. In truth, the raceway was probably significantly altered to accommodate additions to the furnace operation.

There are apparently no surviving records of the size of the original furnace until 1831, when it was rebuilt. The dimensions after it was rebuilt were nine feet wide by thirty-three feet high inside.[140] This was also likely the stack size before it was rebuilt. For many centuries, this was considered to be the optimal size for a charcoal furnace. If a charcoal furnace was built much higher, the weight of the charge would be too great, causing it to collapse in on itself. This would restrict the flow of oxygen, which in turn would lower the temperature or simply require more time and fuel to reach the required temperature of three thousand degrees Fahrenheit for the smelting of iron. In the opposite case, if a furnace was too short, it would not efficiently use the heat it produced. For these reasons, in addition to the fact that records state that the yield of the Catoctin Furnace stack did not significantly change after it was rebuilt, it would seem that the furnace did not change in size with this rebuilding.[141]

The furnace at Catoctin, like most charcoal furnaces of that era, was built of stone, with a square base about twenty-five feet wide that slowly tapered until it was about sixteen or eighteen feet wide at the top. The inside dimension of thirty-three feet can be assumed to be the height of the furnace above ground level. Although there was a significant foundation under charcoal furnaces to support their weight, the height above ground could not be greater than the inside height, as the inside height was the measurement from the very top hole, where the furnace was charged, to ground level, where the opening to emit molten iron and slag was located.

The inside of a charcoal furnace looked like a lamp chimney. It was circular throughout its entire height, measuring approximately eighteen inches in diameter at the top, where the charge was applied, and slowly increasing in diameter toward the bottom until it reached a full width of approximately nine feet about two-thirds of the way down from the top. It then tapered in rapidly, to a width of about two feet, and remained roughly this width for the bottom five feet. This was the crucible. On one side of the furnace, usually considered the front, there was a hearth. At the base of the furnace, there was a small door leading into the crucible. The molten iron and slag poured out from this door. Slag, the byproduct of iron manufacturing, was taken off every few hours from the upper half of the door. Charcoal furnaces were usually tapped for iron every twelve hours, and there is no reason to think that Catoctin was any different.

A charcoal furnace the size of the original Catoctin Furnace required roughly an acre of hard wood for every twenty-four hours of operation. The wood had to be made into charcoal by means of a lengthy process performed by very skilled men called colliers.

In order to provide wood to make charcoal, iron furnaces always possessed large tracts of timberland. In the case of Catoctin Furnace, a tract of land varying in size from 4,600 to 11,000 acres provided wood for coaling during its one and a quarter centuries of operation. Teams of woodcutters would enter a selected area, cut the timber into four-foot lengths and discard the

Illustration of the charcoal-making process and colliers at work constructing a charcoal mound prior to burning. *Photograph in the collection of the Catoctin Furnace Historical Society, original work not identified.*

An ore cart, used for transporting raw ore to the furnace. *Photograph courtesy of the collection of Mary Rae Cantwell.*

brush in piles near where it was cut. The lengths of wood were split, if necessary, into pieces not larger than roughly six inches in diameter. They were then piled on stacks to await the colliers, who would convert the wood into charcoal.[142]

Once the coaling operation was completed and the charcoal had cooled down, it had to be delivered to the furnace. Large mule-drawn wagons were used for this. The charcoal was scooped into large baskets, which in turn were dumped into the mule wagon. When the wagon arrived at the furnace, the charcoal was again scooped into baskets and dumped into a large charcoal storage shed.[143] When the shed was empty, charcoal was dumped in at ground level; however, if the shed had a large quantity of charcoal in it, additional charcoal was deposited through openings near the top. Because the charcoal was so light in weight, large quantities could be moved at once. Therefore, the charcoal wagon was large, as mule wagons go. Once the charcoal had arrived at the furnace, it was ready to be used in the process of making iron.

The ore needed to operate Catoctin Furnace in the early years was taken from a small mine bank within 100 feet of the furnace.[144] This bank reached a size of 300 feet by 125 feet and a depth of 30 feet.[145] When the operation was small, only small quantities of ore were needed. Ore was generally carried to the furnace by mule carts and stored in the bridge house so that it would be readily accessible.

As the operation grew, different mine banks were opened at greater distances from the furnace. A second bank was opened approximately half a mile southwest of the furnace stack. At its greatest capacity, it reached a size of five hundred by two hundred feet and a depth of twenty feet.[146] Ore was carried from this bank to the furnace stack on a mule-powered railroad.

In this open-pit mine, railroad tracks were laid into the side of the hill so that the mule cart could be backed right under the area where the miners were removing the ore. As they dug, the ore simply fell into the carts. There is an existing photograph of this operation.

Around the middle of the nineteenth century, a third pit, which would become the largest of them, was opened. By the time this pit was abandoned, it had reached a length of two thousand feet and a width of several hundred feet, with a depth of at least forty feet.[147] The vast majority of the ore that

Open Mine Bank (Ore Pit) south of the furnace, showing mule-drawn ore carts on primitive rails, circa 1895. *Photograph attributed to William L. Renner, in the Carl E. Brown collection, courtesy of the Maryland Room, Frederick County Public Libraries.*

Upper Mine Bank (Catoctin Ore Bank), circa 1906, after the introduction of the Vulcan steam shovel with Dinky (ore) railroad engine to the right of the shovel. *Photograph courtesy of the Catoctin Furnace Historical Society.*

was removed from this pit was taken out with steam-powered shovels that crawled on railroad tracks. It was hauled out of the mine banks by a small steam engine.

All ore that was used in the Catoctin Furnace had to be washed to remove impurities. The washing was accomplished by dumping the ore into a trough through which water from a natural stream flowed. The water carried away the light soil and left the heavier ore. This was usually done near the mine banks instead of at the furnace site to lessen the amount of material that had to be carried to the furnace. All the ores mined at Catoctin Furnace were brown hematite. This ore did not contain large quantities of sulfur or other such impurities and therefore did not have to be heated for purification before it was used in the furnace.

The final product needed for the manufacture of iron is limestone, which is called *flux* in a furnace. It is used in the smelting of iron as a receiving agent for the impurities that are released from the iron ore. Limestone is a base and therefore has a pH above seven. The impurities of iron ore are acidic and therefore have a pH of seven or below. When the limestone is added, it will combine with the acidic impurities and neutralize them so that they may be separated as slag from the iron.

Philip T. Tyson, in his *Second Report of the State Agricultural Chemist*, reported:

> *In smelting iron ores at the Catoctin furnaces an oxide of zinc constantly accumulates near the upper part of the furnaces, (called the tunnel head), indicating the presence of that metal either in the iron ore or limestone used.*[148]

Throughout the operation of Catoctin Furnace, limestone was acquired from three basic locations. In the early years, a limestone quarry within several hundred yards of the furnace provided the small amount needed. In 1872, the Western Maryland Railroad was completed from Thurmont to Hagerstown, making it easy to ship limestone (to be used as flux) across the mountain. In this time period, Catoctin Furnace began to acquire its limestone from the P.G. Zouck and Co. quarry in Cavetown.[149] This limestone was high in magnesium.

Shortly after this, in 1876, John Baker Kunkel, the owner of Catoctin Furnace, applied for a patent with the United States Patent Office that described how he felt he could improve the quality of iron by using high magnesium limestone as flux.[150] It was believed that magnesium, which has a high affinity for phosphorus, would pick up or combine with the phosphorus that was a naturally occurring impurity within early irons and remove it along with the slag. The removal of phosphorus from iron makes the iron harder or less brittle. Leonard R. Waesche, who was a managerial employee of John Baker Kunkel and later managed the furnace, stated that "no notable results seemed to follow the granting of this patent, but it shows that he [Kunkel] was running his plant intelligently."[151]

In 1900, when the furnace was restarted after an eight-year shutdown, limestone was acquired from Spahr's Quarry, which was situated approximately two miles south of the furnace.[152] This limestone was hauled on the Frederick Railroad until 1903, when the furnace shut down for the final time.

Once these three commodities were on site, the furnace could be charged and iron made. The charcoal fuel was needed in larger quantities than ore and limestone. After the furnace was started, it was recharged about every half hour. At these chargings, a quantity of about fifteen bushels of charcoal, four hundred pounds of ore and forty pounds of limestone was used.[153] These figures could vary significantly, according to the quality of the ore. If the ore was of a poorer grade, it was necessary to use more ore and, subsequently, more limestone to pick up the impurities. However, if the ore was of high quality, less ore and less limestone would be needed.

The iron ore and the limestone were stored in the bridge house so that they would be readily accessible for the charging of the furnace. However, the charcoal was stored a short distance away for two reasons: its volume was too great to store in the bridge house, and it would be a fire hazard if stored near the furnace.

When the furnace was put into blast, it usually stayed in blast for many months, only being shut down when necessity required it. One of the main reasons for shutting down Catoctin Furnace, or any iron furnace, was a shortage or complete lack of one of the materials needed in its charge. If the operation ran out of charcoal due to the fact that the colliers were unable to keep up because of bad weather or some other reason, the furnace would have to be shut down or "blown out."

Another reason for shutting down could have been a lack of the water required to run the blast. In the wintertime, Little Hunting Creek would occasionally freeze. There are also reports of drought forcing the furnace to be shut down in the summer.[154] A final reason for shutting down the furnace would have been the deterioration of the lining.

When a furnace is built, a permanent lining of basic brick is built into the wall at a thickness of approximately two to three feet.[155] This is actually a sub lining, and it should never have to be removed until the furnace is dismantled. A final lining of a very tough material is then put into place. Because of the three-thousand-degree-Fahrenheit temperatures and the constant wear on this material, it must be replaced at frequent intervals. This final lining was installed from the inside by workers who entered the furnace from the top and/or bottom. The material that was best suited for this purpose during most of the era of Catoctin Furnace was magnesium.[156] However, due to cost and availability, the next best material, dolomite, was usually used.[157] Whether magnesium or dolomite is used is of little consequence to the overall function of the furnace. Both materials have virtually the same qualities and reactions under the stress of an iron furnace's operations.

In order for a furnace lining to be adequate, it had to have several qualities. It had to be able to withstand the highest temperatures that the furnace would reach; in other words, it had to be refractory above three thousand degrees Fahrenheit so that it would not melt off into the charge. The lining had to withstand the corrosive action of the slag and iron and also had to avoid disintegration when the furnace cooled down. The material used for lining had to avoid cracking when heated to high temperatures, and it had to have sufficient strength to withstand the sloshing of molten ore and slag within the furnace. Finally, the material had to be inexpensive and readily available.[158] This was especially true in the early days of Catoctin Furnace, since transportation was difficult. Fire-resistant stone was hauled from near the mouth of the Monocacy River to Catoctin Furnace by horse and wagon to be used for lining.[159]

The founder or his assistant, the keeper, controlled the operation of the furnace by dictating the amounts used of charcoal, iron and flux, as well as their proportions to one another. They knew when the furnace was ready to be tapped by the color of the molten iron and its texture. The founder could observe this by looking through the side of the furnace, where the tuyere was inserted. An iron bar could also be inserted through a hole in the door and then extracted. By observing the iron that clung to the bar, the founder could determine the separation of the iron and slag. It was also important to watch the top of the furnace stack in order to determine the condition of the charge inside.

Controlling the condition of the charge within the furnace is the most important part of iron manufacturing. By adjusting the blast and the proportions of charcoal, ore and flux, the founder not only controlled the quality of the iron but also prevented the furnace from freezing up. If a disastrous mistake was made and molten ore and slag were allowed to cool below melting point before they were discharged from the bottom of the furnace, they could, and most likely would, set up. This is called "freezing up." The reason that this is such a disaster is that once it happens, the only way to remove the solidified charge is to dismantle the furnace. It is important to mention that there is no record of this ever occurring at Catoctin Furnace. Most mention made of freezing up is usually concerned with an attempt to seriously modify the design of a furnace to change the nature or type of fuel used in its operations.

Once the iron reached the level of separation or quality desired, the furnace was tapped. Two things were usually done with the iron, depending on its quality and on market demand. Lower-quality iron was usually allowed to run out of the furnace and down a trough on a sloping, sandy floor. From this trough, there were extensions cut into the floor to both the right and the left. These troughs were about two feet long and three to four inches wide and had depths roughly equal to their widths. The main trough was called a *sow*, with side troughs called *pigs*; the assemblage was named thus due to its unusual shape, which was similar to that of a nursing sow. When the iron had finished flowing down the main trough into the pigs and

Furnace gutter man, while tapping the furnace. *Original woodcut courtesy of the estate of Constantine Kermes.*

Artist's rendition of the furnace-tapping process, producing pig iron. *Photograph in the collection of the Catoctin Furnace Historical Society, original work not identified.*

FOUNDER
CASTING IRON

© Constantine Kermes '68

An iron founder at work pouring molten iron into a mold. *Original woodcut courtesy of the estate of Constantine Kermes.*

solidified, it was sold as iron bars, hence the term "pig iron." It was used by foundries and blacksmiths to manufacture iron items.

Iron of higher quality was usually ladled out into molds made of sand and wood. The general shape was a wooden box split in two through the middle and filled with sand. A wooden pattern was made in the shape of the item to be molded, put between the two halves of the mold and pressed. When the wood was removed, the shape of the item to be made was imprinted in the sand. The two halves of the box were then fitted together, leaving a hollow area for the molten iron to fill. The iron was poured into the mold through a hole left in the side of the box for this purpose. Once the molded iron had cooled and was removed from the mold, the small extension through which the iron had flowed into the mold had to be removed. The finished product sometimes required buffing or sanding to improve its surface quality. Everything from pots and pans to cannon barrels was manufactured through this process. At Catoctin Furnace, the main products of molding were pots, pans and stove plates. If molding was done improperly, the result could be a worthless product. The shells that the Johnson brothers manufactured for the Revolutionary War are good examples of improper casting or molding and the results it can bring.

As time passed, new innovations were added to the iron industry, first in Britain and then in the United States. In the years shortly after Catoctin Furnace was built, the principle of hot blast was invented in Britain. The term "hot blast" means that the air used in the furnace blast is heated before it is blown into the furnace. The purpose of this is to help prevent the air from being a constant cooling factor working against the efforts to melt the iron ore. This technique was originally used in Britain in an effort to try to smelt iron with coal, which burns at a lower temperature than charcoal. It was soon found that hot blast greatly increased the efficiency of charcoal furnaces.

By 1831, when the owner of Catoctin Furnace, John Brien, had to rebuild the original furnace due to deterioration, it was likely converted to hot blast.[160] Throughout the rest of its years of operation, it was listed as a hot-blast water-powered furnace. It is difficult to know the actual capacity of the furnace, as reports vary from 1,000 to 2,500 tons annually.

In 1857, Peregrine Fitzhugh, the owner at the time, built a second stack of the same size alongside the original. This stack, known as Isabella, was built as a cold-blast steam-operated furnace.[161] By this period, steam technology had progressed to such a point that industry was using it in many capacities. At Catoctin Furnace, the advantages of using steam to run the blast gave this furnace the ability to operate when water would otherwise not be able to provide blast due to freezing or drought.

Most likely, the second stack was cold blast due to the fact that it was inconvenient to have both a hot blast and steam power in one charcoal unit. The heat required to warm the blast or make steam is generally acquired by mounting boilers or some form of a heat box on top of the furnace so that its surplus heat can be used as the heat source.

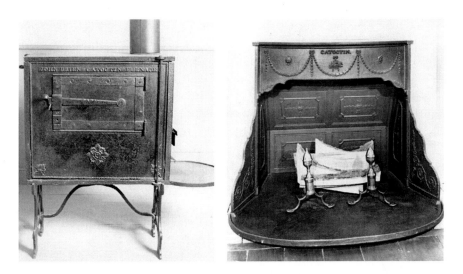

Left: A John Brien plate stove manufactured at Catoctin Furnace, in the collection of Old Salem, Inc. *Photography courtesy of Old Salem, Inc.*

Right: A Franklin stove manufactured at Catoctin Furnace, in the collection of Old Salem, Inc. *Photography courtesy of Old Salem, Inc.*

Catoctin Furnace operated these two charcoal units from 1857 until 1873, at a maximum annual capacity of around five thousand tons,[162] although the actual production was most likely lower due to downtime for such reasons as relining.

In 1873, owner John Baker Kunkel installed a coal coke furnace. This furnace had an inside dimension of fifty by eleven and a half feet and was built in a steel case with the same type of lining as those inside the charcoal furnaces. This unit, being much more modern, was both hot blast and steam powered and had an annual capacity of about six thousand tons.[163] Coke furnaces such as this one were no longer built into banks with a bridge house from which to charge them. Instead, they were equipped with large elevators to raise the fuel and the iron ore to the top of the stack. The fuel for this furnace, called Connellsville coke, was brought from Connellsville, Pennsylvania, by railroad to Thurmont and then hauled to Catoctin Furnace by wagons until 1886, when the Monocacy Valley Railroad was completed to Catoctin Furnace.

Coke, which is pre-burned bituminous coal, was prepared and marketed to iron furnaces as an alternative to charcoal fuel. Charcoal was becoming extremely expensive to make due to higher labor costs and depletion of the forests around iron furnaces.

This third and final furnace at Catoctin, Deborah, operated from 1874 until 1892, at an annual capacity of 6,000 tons. In 1900, when the furnace was reopened after an eight-year period of shutdown, the height of the Deborah furnace was raised to sixty-five feet, and its daily capacity was increased from the previous 35 tons to 40 tons.[164] It operated at this capacity until the furnace was shut down for the final time in 1903. In 1894, when this stack was sitting idle, it was one of only five coal coke stacks in the state of Maryland. Four of these stacks were owned by Maryland Steel and situated in Sparrows Point, Maryland. They had an annual capacity of 358,000 tons, were fueled with coke from the Appalachian region and used ore from Cuba, Spain and Africa.[165] The vast difference in the capacity of these four furnaces compared to that of the one at Catoctin Furnace suggests one of the key reasons that Catoctin Furnace was becoming difficult to operate profitably.

In 1906, Catoctin Furnace was sold for the final time as an iron furnace to Joseph Thropp. He removed the Deborah furnace and all other valuable items from the area and hauled them to his Bedford County, Pennsylvania operation. This brought an end to the era of iron manufacturing in Frederick County, Maryland, as Catoctin Furnace went the way of all small iron furnaces.

Chapter 5
THE BLACK POPULATION

B lack slaves provided a large part of the labor force at Catoctin Furnace in the early days. It was common policy for slave labor to be used in iron manufacture, particularly in the South. For a little over half a century, the owners of Catoctin Furnace followed this course in their operation.

The Johnson brothers, as part of an aristocratic colonial society, had extensive slaveholdings. Slave labor was used both in the iron-working partnership and individually on Johnson manors. In a bill of sale dated November 27, 1788, Thomas, James, Baker and Roger Johnson bought the possessions of John Rawlings, an ironmaster who had worked with James at Catoctin. Among the possessions listed were four slaves: a thirty-five-year-old man named Jack; two boys, eighteen-year-old Jaines and thirteen-year-old Phil; and Phil's mother, Milly, aged thirty-seven.[166]

The role of slave labor as an integral part of the iron operation is described in the diary of John Frederick Schlegel, minister to the Graceham Moravian congregation. Writing of his activities of July 30, 1799, Brother Schlegel said that he paid a visit to James Johnson and his brother(s) and sons. He particularly visited with the "poor Negroes" at the furnace whom he described as being inwardly and outwardly troubled by their conditions. They gathered around him at the furnace stack weeping at his words of comfort. They told him that they had to work seven days a week in the iron smelter (furnace) and seldom could hear the Word of God. As he finished talking to them, "the signal was given for the pour," and each of them had to be back at work.[167]

In 1827, when Moravian clergymen started holding services at Catoctin, they regularly found blacks, as well as whites, in their congregation. They also visited and ministered to blacks in their homes. One of the greatest sources of joy to the Moravians was the opportunity to bring divine guidance to blacks, who were described as being in the majority among furnace workers and had no other chance to hear the Gospel. Some of these people must have been elderly because they are described as having iron-gray hair.[168]

In 1800, James Johnson owned more than seventy slaves, many of whom were employed on the manor, while some helped at the furnace and at Johnson's Bush Creek Forge.[169] Thomas Johnson was the fourth-largest slave owner in Frederick County in 1790, having thirty-eight slaves.[170] In his 1809 will, Baker Johnson listed his slaves by name and family. He owned approximately eighty slaves, whom he divided at his death among his wife and eight children. Some of these slaves obviously were experienced in phases of iron making, having been trained in their native countries to make iron products. Their roles at the furnace were clearly stated in Johnson's will as Collier Sam and Waggoners Henry and Harvey.[171] Baker Johnson also

The stone mule barn at Catoctin Furnace, photographed during the late nineteenth century or early twentieth century. *Photograph courtesy of Mary Rae Cantwell, now in the collection of the Catoctin Furnace Historical Society.*

owned a vineyard where some of his blacks worked. The Catoctin slaves probably lived in some of the cottages provided by the furnace owner.[172]

Black youths learned various trades from experienced black craftsmen. They became blacksmiths, colliers, founders and forge men. At times, black women assisted in the iron complex operation, helping out in charcoal making or working in the ore pits. One advantage of having a large number of slaves was the presence of a reliable workforce. The owners did not have to bother with hiring or with dealing with workers who moved on to other jobs.[173]

At the beginning of the nineteenth century, the price of skilled slaves rose, reaching a peak of £80 to £100. In addition, the owner had to provide all the necessities for the slaves, which added to their cost. As free labor became more plentiful, it was cheaper to hire workers for a yearly wage of £15 to £16.[174]

The older Johnson generation died out, but the practice of slaveholding continued. In 1820, James Johnson Jr. owned sixty-six slaves at Springfield. One free black male also worked for him. Twenty of these slaves were involved in farming, sixteen of them were females who helped with running the household and the balance were children.[175] By 1820, Baker Johnson Jr., who inherited thirteen slaves from his father, had increased his holdings to twenty-six. The adult males worked the land at Auburn. Two members of the Johnson household were working in manufacturing, probably at the ironworks, but there is no indication that they were black.[176]

Benjamin Blackford had a number of black workers at Catoctin and later at Isabella Furnace in Virginia. They referred to him as "Old Master," so they probably were slaves who had been with him for some time and went with him when he left Catoctin.[177] While living in Virginia, Blackford and his wife were active in the movement to return the slaves to Africa.[178] Blackford's successor, Willoughby Mayberry, borrowed money in 1819 against his personal possessions. He listed one slave, a man named Daniel, who was between twenty and thirty years old.[179] The following year, the census indicated that Daniel had married, for Mayberry had a slave couple working in his household.[180]

John Brien owned and employed a number of slaves, as indicated by the Moravian clergy reports of 1820 to 1834. These people worked on Auburn manor as well as in the furnace operation. Brien's sons, Henry and John McPherson Brien, also owned slaves. Five of Henry's slaves worked in the ore mines.[181] The largest number of John McPherson Brien's slaves was at Antietam Ironworks in Washington County. In 1841, he had a workforce of two hundred whites and sixty slaves. He was reported to be a kind master whose slaves were better cared for and happier than free Negroes.[182] However, the blacks seemed to feel differently. On June 12, 1848, John McPherson Brien wrote to his attorney in Baltimore concerning some of his financial difficulties. He said that there was a "good deal of dissatisfaction among the Negroes" arising as a result of a property sale. Many of the blacks had gone to Brien to express their unwillingness to remain with him, and he was astonished, for in his words:

> *I had always treated them most kindly, this is, indeed, gross ingratitude. What would you advise me to do with those who have shown such ungratefulness? It would be a serious loss to me, if they would leave... for Pennsylvania.*[183]

John McPherson Jr. seemed to have held a different view of the slave situation from that of his nephew John McPherson Brien. In May 1831, Dr. Eli Ayres, of the Maryland State Colonization Society, visited Frederick with the hope of establishing an auxiliary society, collecting funds and signing up manumitted slaves who wished to return to Africa. John McPherson Jr. served as treasurer of the Frederick County Auxiliary Society. Dr. Ayres was very optimistic, stating that those owners who had manumitted their slaves and hired whites were well satisfied. His success was not great among blacks, however. Many mistrusted him, believing he was a Georgia slave dealer. Not one Frederick County black was among the thirty-one who sailed on board the *Orion* for Africa in October 1831. During the years it was in operation, the society enjoyed only limited success in Frederick County, sending sixty-six blacks to Liberia.[184]

By mid-century, the number of slaves had declined sharply in the Catoctin area. William Johnson, son of Baker Sr., owned seven, and James Schley owned fifteen slaves. These slaves worked on their farms. Also, Dr. William McPherson, the young physician at Catoctin, had three slaves, two male and one female, all under twenty-two years of age, and Peregrine Fitzhugh owned eight, four of whom were children. Only one, a forty-year-old woman, was over twenty-one. More than likely, these were household servants.[185] The Episcopal clergyman at Harriet Chapel in Catoctin Furnace baptized the black children. The 1854 report of the Reverend James A. Harrell included two colored infants baptized,[186] and the 1856 report also listed two colored infant baptisms.[187]

The burial place of many area blacks is a small cemetery on a hill about a half mile south of the furnace. Here, in graves marked by only

A Mid-Atlantic Archaeological Research, Inc. crew at work during the 1981 study of the Catoctin Furnace slave cemetery. *Photograph courtesy of the Catoctin Furnace Historical Society.*

an occasional field stone, are the remains of men, women and children. A recent anthropological investigation of the cemetery revealed some one hundred graves or possible grave sites.[188] The bodies excavated were found to be of blacks, first- or second-generation arrivals from Africa. In some cases, the bodies were grouped in what appeared to be family plots. Most of the coffins were of the "pinch-toe" type, of simple slat construction and held together with various kinds of nails, both hand wrought and machine cut. The presence of some buttons or shroud pins indicates the individuals were buried in simple clothing or shrouds. There was no jewelry or other grave goods found, only the remains of several fruit and leaf funeral wreaths. The burials were made starting in the late eighteenth century and lasted well into the nineteenth century. No trace has been found to date of an iron coffin that folklore indicates contained the body of a mountain-dwelling mulatto who was a victim of smallpox.[189]

Chapter 6

THE WORKER AND FAMILY LIFE

At Catoctin Furnace, the backbone of the plant was the furnace worker who provided the muscle and sweat to achieve the goals of the planner and financier of the iron industry. Coming from a variety of backgrounds and performing a variety of tasks, the worker was part of a plantation system. He lived in company housing, bought from the company store and even attended a church provided by the company owner.[190] His home life was simple but made interesting by a variety of lively entertainment. For him, life revolved around "the Furnace."

When James Johnson started the ironworking business, he needed a variety of labor, both skilled and unskilled. Slave labor accounted for a goodly portion of the workforce in the early period.[191] Other workers came from a variety of backgrounds. Some were immigrants, some were from neighboring states and some were natives of Maryland. By the middle of the nineteenth century, free labor appears to have been a more significant component. In 1845 an advertisement in the Baltimore *Sun* sought laborers and pattern-makers for the Catoctin Furnace.[192]

One of the earliest workers about whom we have information was John Rawlings, an ironmaster. Rawlings came to Catoctin from Virginia, bringing his slaves with him. On November 27, 1788, Rawlings sold the slaves, a horse and household possessions to the four Johnson brothers, operators of the Catoctin iron complex, and moved on.[193]

Among the workers in the early nineteenth century was William Simpson, native of County Antrim, Ireland, who immigrated to Maryland in 1818.

He became acquainted with Luke Tiernan of Baltimore, a commission merchant and fervent Irish Catholic. Tiernan was the father of Ann Tiernan Brien. Simpson came to Catoctin Furnace to work for John Brien. At the time of his death in 1828, Simpson's quarters were described as a "miserable" hut by Brother Reinke, the Moravian clergyman who held Simpson's funeral.[194] Simpson recalled the brothers and sisters he had left in Ireland and willed to them his estate of approximately $600.[195]

Following in Simpson's footsteps, a trickle of emigrants from Ireland early in the nineteenth century soon became a flood. Starvation and disease following the potato blight in 1845 drove thousands of Irish from their native land. Many of them found employment as manual laborers in industries like the ironworks at Catoctin. Among the new Irish workers were John Fitzgerald; his wife, Mary; and their sons, John and James. The three men worked in the iron mine, along with many others of their native country. Of the many Irishmen who became iron miners, we know of John Cunningham, Robert Hammader, James Noble, John Conley, Edward Ross, Michael Brice, Thomas Cairy, John Russell, Michael Conner, Patrick McGill, Patrick Cain, Thomas Gelvin, John Cramer, Anthony Coil, Thomas Sullivan, James Crosby and James O'Conner.[196] A few miners were natives of Germany, namely George Freshman, George Andrews, Peter Flexanhart and John Knetts.

In addition to the workmen needed in the mines, a large number of men were employed as charcoal workers. Often the collier was assisted by his son, as in the case of Joseph Davis and his son Josiah, and John Hippinsteel and James, his son and assistant.[197] The first step in making charcoal was cutting the wood. Woodcutting on the furnace mountain land was a way to make extra money when work was slow. Much of the cutting was done in the winter. The wood was cut in four-foot lengths and ranked in cords in preparation for the charcoal-burning operation. The underbrush was laid aside, and as it dried, it created a serious fire hazard. Mountain fires were a common result of burning charcoal close to dry underbrush. One such disaster occurred on April 18, 1826, when a fire broke out in a brush pile started from embers fanned by high wind. The fire raged for three days, causing much damage. In spite of the efforts of all who went to fight it, the fire burned until it had consumed three thousand cords of furnace wood, as well as thousands of fence rails and bark for tanners. The loss was estimated at four or five thousand dollars.[198]

The charcoal collier and his assistants lived in a crude circular hut while they worked in the woods. The hut was built of slanted poles that stood

A collier's hut, from a National Park Service demonstration in Catoctin Mountain Park. The hut is a permanent exhibit on the Charcoal Trail. *Photograph courtesy of the Catoctin Furnace Historical Society.*

"tepee style" and were covered with leaves and earth. It was reasonably warm and watertight.

Each burning crew leveled a space known as "the pit." Wood that had been previously cut was hauled to the pits to be burned. Men like Samuel Jamison were wood haulers. The next step was to build a frame around which kindling could be piled. A pole about four inches in diameter was stood up in the center of the frame. Next, the cordwood was stood on end around the frame, forming a cone-shaped pile about thirty feet in diameter at the bottom and as much as ten feet high at the top. The pile was covered with leaves and dirt, making it airtight. As soon as one pit was finished, another was started. When the time came for the firing, the center pole was removed and fire was dropped down the hole, lighting the kindling at the bottom. The collier had to be very skillful to control the fire. Some draft was needed to keep the fire alive, but too much draft burned the wood to ashes. The fire had to be held to a smoldering stage. The coaling process took about twelve days, followed by a four-day cooling-off period.[199] During that time, watch had to be kept day and

The charcoal burn process, after construction of the stack is completed and the stack is about to be fired. From the National Park Service collier demonstration. *Photograph courtesy of the Catoctin Furnace Historical Society.*

night. When the coal from the pit was cool, word was sent to the furnace so that the mule-drawn charcoal wagon could start hauling the finished charcoal. When the wagon arrived, the coal was loaded into large woven hickory baskets. Men carried the baskets over their heads and dumped them into their charcoal wagon. Charcoal was stored in the stack house at the furnace until it was needed.

Some of the people involved in the coaling operation while John Baker Kunkel was furnace owner were: Yancey May and his son John and brothers Josiah and Joshua Miller, who were woodchoppers; Jonathon Frailey and David Martin, who worked in the colliery; William Shuff, John Davis, James Penwell, Jacob Sweeney, Edward Giles, Chris Nunemaker, Joseph Davis and John Hippensteel, who were colliers; and James Jamison, Philip Jamison and Philip's son Isaiah, who were charcoal rakers. The mule teams were driven by John Jamison, Samuel Mozinge, Thomas Martin, Joseph Martin and Jacob Nunemaker.[200]

As the iron ore was brought from the ore banks, it was first washed and then transported to the furnace. In the early days, the ore carts were pulled by mules, but later a "dinky" engine helped with this task. Part of the trip from mine to furnace was downhill. In the days when mules were still being used, the mule was unhitched and led to the back of the carrier, where he stepped up on a platform and rode to the bottom of the grade along with the load of washed ore.[201] When the ore cart was dumped, the mule was ready to pull it back to the ore bank.

Limestone was needed as flux in the furnace to carry off impurities remaining after the melting process. These impurities formed part of the slag that was dumped in huge heaps around Catoctin Furnace. Limestone deposits were located near the furnace. Among the men who worked in the limestone quarry were Henry Woolard and Robert Shuff.[202]

The furnace founder was responsible for the success of the operation. Freeman Traver, a native of New York, was founder for Peregrine Fitzhugh.[203] In 1870, Catoctin's founder was John Holtz, a native of Prussia.[204] The founder adjusted the blast, kept an eye on the flame and gases emerging from the furnace and decided when the furnace was ready to tap. He was also responsible for the molds and trenches, or the sows and the pigs into which pig iron flowed. A good founder could tell the state of the smelting by the color of the molten mass.

The founder's assistant was known as the keeper. Often, the keeper ran the furnace when the founder was not there, especially at night. Keepers worked in shifts. In 1870, Solomon Penwell, Thomas Benner, Ballard Murry and Martin Miller were keepers at Catoctin. William Weddle helped out in the pouring, working as a gutter man. His responsibility was to carry away the slag that came out when the furnace was tapped. Another highly skilled worker was the molder, who carefully formed sand molds into which molten iron was poured to make such products as stove plates and fire backs. Thomas Frailey worked as a molder.[205]

Part of the operation under John Baker Kunkel involved forge work. The forge men were Nash Camp, John Pogue and Gilbert Hoover. In 1879, Kunkel also employed a manager, George Ott; a clerk, John Dykes; and an ironmaster, John Hoover. Others having specialized jobs connected with the operation were Israel Sweeney and his son Thomas, both of whom were carpenters; John, William and Charles Weddle and Nelson Freshour, blacksmiths; and John Hellman and William Stoner, who ran steam engines.[206]

The products of Catoctin Furnace had to be hauled to Frederick or Thurmont to be shipped by rail until a railroad was laid to the furnace in 1886. A large part of this hauling was handled by local farmers, who were paid $1.50 per ton. Sometimes they hauled as much as twenty-four to thirty tons a week. Pig iron and iron castings were hauled to town for sale or shipment. On the return trip, store and furnace supplies were brought to Catoctin Furnace. Lumber, bricks, flour, salt, sugar, molasses, bacon, potatoes, stove coal and even furniture were hauled. The farm wagons also hauled limestone from the local quarry.[207]

Workers moved back and forth between iron operations as work was available. The family of Solomon Penwell, furnace keeper, was in Maryland in 1853 and 1854, when James and Jonathon were born; in Pennsylvania in 1857, when William arrived; back in Maryland from 1860 to 1864 for the births of Margaret and George; and in Pennsylvania again from 1865 to 1867, when Robert and Samuel were born. They were in Maryland in 1870.[208]

For some, getting to the job was another difficult task. Charles Deitz walked from Wardensville, West Virginia, in about 1870 to work at Catoctin. Later, he moved on to Pennsylvania following jobs.[209] Many of the workers, both foreign and native born, settled in the area and remained after the furnace shut down. Richard Kelly, the clerk in the company store, was born

A Catoctin Village streetscape in the mid-twentieth century. *Photograph courtesy of Elizabeth Anderson Comer, in the collection of the Catoctin Furnace Historical Society.*

An example of the Catoctin workers' housing, a double log house currently owned by the Catoctin Furnace Historical Society, Inc. *Photograph by A. Aubrey Bodine, copyright Jennifer B. Bodine and courtesy of www.aaubreybodine.com.*

in Ireland.[210] He married a young woman from Pennsylvania and settled in the Catoctin area, where he operated a store for many years.[211] Samuel Reed, who was born in Pennsylvania, bought furnace housing, as did many families, when it became available in the early part of the twentieth century.[212] Prices ranged from around $250 to $450.

The iron plantation provided housing for its workers. While the complex was operated by the Johnsons, between fifteen and twenty stone or log houses were built.[213] Other owners continued to add to this number until, in 1888, there were eighty workers' cottages. In 1899, the average rental rate for the houses was two to four dollars per month.[214] Part of the understanding about living in company housing was that the building would be whitewashed each spring by the thirtieth of May. The residents did not spare the whitewash. They covered the house, outbuildings, picket fences and, during "spring cleaning," set their furnishings aside and whitewashed the houses' interiors. The ceilings were not enclosed, so getting whitewash applied to the laths and underside of the wooden shingled roof was a messy task. After the whitewash was applied, the floors were scrubbed with a brush, using lye soap.[215]

Furniture in the workers' houses was very simple compared to the luxury of the ironmaster's house. An 1823 bill of sale listed the belongings of James Shuff, including two beds with bedding, a table, a corner cupboard, a chest, three chairs, a bench, a cradle, pots and pans, six plates, knives, forks and spoons and miscellaneous tools.[216] A similar bill of sale from the same year listed many similar furnishings of John Moser, including "chaff beds and

(A page from a handwritten ledger is reproduced here, headed "Catoctin Furnaces. Month of [December] 1899 190__   Time for Upper Ore Bank" with a "CREDIT" section. The columns list worker names and daily time marks with monetary amounts; the handwriting is largely illegible.)

Above: A page from the *Upper Mine Ledger,* dated December 1899, showing worker wages and expenditures. *Donated by William Green to the author, original now in the collection of the Historical Society of Frederick County, Inc. archives.*

Right: The company store and office of the Blue Mountain Iron and Steel Company, 1899–1903. *Photograph courtesy of the Catoctin Furnace Historical Society.*

The F.W. Fraley Store, Catoctin, Maryland, circa the late nineteenth century or first quarter of the twentieth century. The Fraley store was subsequently expanded. *Photograph courtesy of the Catoctin Furnace Historical Society.*

bedding."[217] The use of chaff or straw ticks in place of mattresses continued for the next century. Each spring, the old straw was emptied, and for ten cents a new batch was bought from a local farmer and the ticks refilled.[218]

Some workers boarded others in their homes. In 1864, the rate for board was twelve and a half cents for each meal.[219] Single workers could also find housing in several nearby boardinghouses.

Using script in place of money, all supplies that workers needed could be bought at the company store. As in the case of house rent, the bill was deducted from wages. In 1899, after working a month averaging two hundred hours at nine cents per hour and paying two dollars house rent, it was not unusual for a man to have a store bill of ten dollars and a take home pay of six dollars.[220]

Typical commodities that the store carried, with their prices as of 1853, were: potatoes, fifty cents a bushel; mackerel, twenty-five cents a dozen; lemons, thirty cents a dozen; vinegar, twenty-five cents a gallon; butter, twelve cents a pound; lamb, seven cents a pound; flour $5.00 a barrel; and herring, $5.50 a barrel.[221] The furnace company also operated a gristmill in Catoctin Furnace to which nearby farmers could bring their grains for grinding. By using his own wheat, the farmer could have flour for five cents per pound. Farmers like Dr. William McPherson brought their grain to

The furniture of Peregrine Fitzhugh (owner of Catoctin Furnace, 1843–58), in the dining room of Auburn, circa 1980. *Photograph courtesy of Mr. and Mrs. C.E. Gardiner.*

the mill to be ground not only for their own use but also to be sold at the company store.[222]

The company store was not only a supplier of goods to all those within the Catoctin Furnace area, but it was also a social center. Here the workers and their families met with one another, exchanging news and gossip. Even though the furnace owner met with his workers from time to time in the course of the daily operation or when they gathered at the store, there was still a great gulf between them. The workers spoke of the owner's house as "the Big House" or "the High House,"[223] indicating the sense of awe that separated them. A listing of the furniture owned by Willoughby Mayberry showed the grandeur of the owner's home compared to that of a worker.[224] Included were

> *a mahogany side board, pair of mahogany knife cases, eight day clock with mahogany case, large dinner table with circular ends, small dining table… piano forte, eleven bedsteads, two looking glasses, two dressing glasses, two bureaus, one wash stand with china basin…twelve fancy and two recess chairs, thirty common chairs, one settee, one book case, one corner*

cupboard…five carpets, two desks…thirty tablecloths, twenty-four towels, seven feather beds, two pair brass andirons.[225]

The list also included fine silver, china and cut glass, as well as many blankets and coverlets.

It was customary for employees to be invited to the Big House during the Christmas holidays. The house was beautifully decorated, and there was often dancing and refreshments. Christmas celebrations included some unique customs. "Kris Kringling" or "Belsnickling" involved dressing in costumes, including masks, and going from house to house singing carols. The singers were invited inside, where they unmasked and were treated with goodies of the season.

Music played an important part in celebrations and entertainment among the furnace families. Fiddle and guitar were brought out, and a lively tune started feet tapping. In spite of uncertain economic times, "Turkey in the Straw," "Fisher's Hornpipe" and "Brickett's Hornpipe" easily dispelled the gloom. No one could resist a catchy tune like:

> *Dog and the cat and*
> *A wasp and a bumblebee;*
> *Pretty little squirrel*
> *With its tail in a curl,*
> *They've all got a wife but me.*[226]

Refreshments were part of celebrations. One particularly intriguing mixture with the very prosaic name "Settin' the Old Hen" involved hot raisins, sugar and corn. This mixture sat for nine days and then was strained or "racked off."[227] It was a potent gloom chaser.

Most of the women in Catoctin Furnace were homemakers. Their work involved a wide variety of tasks, from gardening and preserving to carrying water, washing, cooking and cleaning. Gardens provided a large part of family food needs. The nearby fields and mountain also yielded game, as well as berries and spring "greens." Many a meal included watercress, rock salad, poke or lamb's quarter. When times really got tight, potatoes were the mainstay of the diet. Using potato and yeast "starter," along with flour and water, great loaves of bread were baked. Potato "pot-pie" was a mixture of cooked potatoes and rolled dough made from flour, salt and water. Occasionally, when they were available, beans were added to the pot.[228] Even though they were far from Ireland,

Photograph of Grandmother Anders (sitting) and an unidentified companion, longtime residents, taken at Catoctin Furnace. *Photograph courtesy of the Catoctin Furnace Historical Society.*

the Irish immigrants felt right at home.

Some women had specialized talents. Mary Jane "Granny" Stitely was the local midwife.[229] She was kept busy; furnace workers had big families.

Many of the immigrant laborers had no opportunity for education. Hard economic times in the early years of the furnace forced young people to work to contribute to the family income. Also, money for books and other necessities connected to school attendance was hard to set aside. After 1868, when the school was built closer to the furnace, it was easier for the children to attend. Most of the families wanted their children to have the opportunity for education, knowing it would lead to better things for them.[230]

Children in Catoctin Furnace lived with an almost constant fireworks display. Flames and gases flickered over the furnace stack, lending an eerie glow to the village at night. When the furnace was charged, sparks and flying ash would rise and settle over everything nearby. There were old test holes, dug to find veins of ore, to jump into. Logging roads in the mountain made wonderful bobsledding trails. Machinery creaked and whined, ore carts sped along the tracks, water rushed in the millrace and over the whole scene a huge copper weather vane, the Indian Sequoia, looked down from the top of the Deborah furnace lift. It was a place to fire the imagination of any child.

Many people from the Catoctin Furnace, Blue Mountain and Mine Bank areas are descendents of one-time furnace workers. It is a tribute to their perseverance that they stayed in the region in spite of severe economic woes when the business closed. They came from hardy stock, putting their mark on the history of the furnace. In turn, the furnace shaped and dominated their lives.

Chapter 7
EDUCATION

The earliest opportunities for education in Frederick County were provided by private schoolmasters in their homes or in classrooms made available by a church or interested citizens. The Moravian congregation in Graceham opened a parochial school in 1758 under the guidance of the pastor. Later, a teacher was hired. This school was in existence for eighty years, until classes were provided under a public school system.[231] Similar arrangements were made by other denominations.

In the case of aristocratic families like the Johnsons, children were tutored at home. When they were older, the young men were sent to private academies or abroad for their educations. Some received training in their chosen professions, such as law, by studying in the office of a practitioner.

Most ironmasters were men of education and culture. They provided their own families with a good education and often made some arrangements for educating the children of employees. The young son of Richard Campbell, clerk of Catoctin ironmaster Willoughby Mayberry, was taught to read by his father. The child spent many happy hours in his father's office at the ironworks. In 1817, the Campbell family left Catoctin after a disagreement with Mayberry over salary. Richard Campbell operated a store in Lewistown, and his son attended school until the following spring, when the father died and the family moved.[232] Within a few years, there was a school at or near Catoctin Furnace. Brother Samuel Reinke of the Moravian church "preached in a schoolhouse" in September 1827.[233]

In 1816, a state school law was enacted providing the Western Shore counties, including Frederick, with a portion of a school fund that was to accumulate until there was enough for a free school in each election district. The state school organization, as set up in 1823, provided for districts and a school tax. In the election of 1826, Frederick County voted to establish a primary school system. The school law of 1837 provided a fund accumulated from investment income, as well as taxation in the county and tuition paid by those able to afford it. This fund supported the early primary schools. Public school education was to be made available to all white children between the ages of five and eighteen.[234]

In August 1839, trustees were elected in the various school districts set up by the Frederick County Board of School Commissioners. Michael Zimmerman, James Schley and William Johnson, son of Baker Sr., were elected in the Furnace District No. 31. In addition, a survey was taken, showing 119 children of school age, for whose education the county provided $107.10, or ninety cents per pupil.[235] The school building was located at the intersection of the Lewistown-to-Mechanicstown Road and the road from Catoctin Furnace to Creagerstown.[236] This particular school remained in use until the districts were relocated and a new school was built closer to Catoctin Furnace in 1868.

The fee for children able to pay their own educational expenses varied according to the year and the length of the session. Summer quarter tuition could be as low as twenty-five cents. Longer winter sessions varied from sixty to ninety cents for each pupil.[237] Only the children who could afford to pay were expected to do so.

The county approved the books to be used in the schools. According to the minutes of February 22, 1841, the Board of Inspectors of Primary Schools disapproved of the introduction into the primary schools of any books that did not show "strict morality, piety and virtue." The commissioners also disapproved of memorizing or reciting any "pieces of composition that do not convey good moral sense and are not in accordance with strict piety and virtue."[238] Teachers were certified as to grade. Those who taught lower grades were required to teach reading, writing, arithmetic, English grammar and geography. Teachers in the next grades were required to teach all of those subjects plus geometry, plane trigonometry and surveying. Students who reached the highest grade were also taught algebra and mensuration.[239]

Residents and employees of Catoctin Furnace served as school trustees: John Weller in 1847 and 1849, Solomon Frailey in 1847 and 1848, Michael Zimmerman in 1849 and 1850, Thomas Frailey in 1850,

Michael Ege in 1852 and William Johnson and Jacob Cronise in 1854.[240] However, the school for District #31 was located several miles from Catoctin Furnace, the growing center of population. This fact sparked interest in educational facilities nearer to the furnace. In March 1850, Harriet A. McPherson, the wife of Dr. William S. McPherson, received a reply to her letter of inquiry about a parochial school.[241] Though no action was taken, the subject did not die. In the 1854 report to the Episcopal Diocese of Maryland, the Reverend James Harrell said that there were few educational advantages in the area. He and "an interested lady"[242] operated a parochial school with twenty-five pupils during the winter, but the effort had to be abandoned because they had no school building. Appeals were made to churches in Baltimore for help, but only $70 was received. This was about one-fifth the amount needed to provide for fifty children.[243] In order to continue the work, Peregrine Fitzhugh offered a large stone house and twenty-five acres of land; but by 1856, only $135 had been contributed, so the money was diverted to other uses in the parish and the plan abandoned.[244] In the fall of 1856, the Reverend Charles M. Parkman showed interest in an offer from Fitzhugh to sell Windy Hill Farm for the establishment of a school. The offer was dropped when it was discovered that Fitzhugh's mother had transferred the farm to another son.[245]

After the school boundaries were redefined in 1866, the owner of the furnace operation, John B. Kunkel and his wife, Deborah, gave the Board of School Commissioners one acre of land for the purpose of building a school.[246] The board set aside $500 to build the new school. During the school year 1869–70, George Williams taught seventy-three scholars. He was paid $200.00 for the fall and winter terms and $94.44 for the spring term. Incidental expenses, including small repairs, were $19.15. Mr. Williams collected $55.73 for book fees, so the cost of running the school for the year was $257.86. Books used in instruction included *McGuffey Readers and Spellers, Brooks' Arithmetic, Cornell's Geographies* and *Tewsmith's Grammar.*[247] The cost of the readers in 1871 was ten cents for the first reader, twenty cents for the second, thirty cents for the third, thirty-five cents for the fourth, fifty-five cents for the fifth, sixty-five cents for the sixth and ten cents for the speller. The treasurer of the school system urged that book fees be collected promptly, believing that the amount collected could be doubled if the teachers took more care in the task. He also chided teachers about allowing children to destroy school property. Most of the incidental expenses were for glass and putty to fix broken windows.[248]

The enrollment varied sharply from year to year. If the financial situation was particularly bad, children worked instead of attending school. At times, book cost must have placed a difficult burden on families, especially those with a number of children. Only fifty-one pupils were enrolled at the Furnace School in 1870–71; and the session must have been very irregular because Duffield Loudon, the teacher, was paid only $55.91 for the fall term and $13.63 for the winter term. In the spring, a new teacher, E.P. Hatcher, had just thirty-one pupils and collected a $75.00 salary. In August 1872, the Reverend James Averitt, who served as a trustee, requested permission to leave Catoctin Parish partly because his children were ready for school and he felt there was nothing for them to attend closer than Frederick.[249] There was a woman, Maggie Benner, teaching in 1875; she taught forty-six pupils, receiving $90.00 for the spring term.

The school built in 1869 on the land donated by the Kunkels was a frame one-room building. It was heated by a stove and had two outhouses in the backyard. Drinking water was carried from a well on land belonging to the furnace owner.[250] It was considered a privilege to be one of a team that went to fetch water. The children carried the full bucket back, each one holding

Photograph of the class of the Catoctin School, December 18, 1911. *Photograph courtesy of the Catoctin Furnace Historical Society.*

the end of a stick stuck through the handle to distribute the weight.[251] The teacher taught seven grades in the one room, sometimes using the help of older students with the little ones. In addition to the books sold at the school, slates, paper tablets and pencils could be bought at the company store.

District #15 did not have a school for blacks. The closest was located in the Creagerstown District. Bella Graham taught twenty-five black students at that school in 1872. The average salary for black teachers was $50 per quarter, compared to an average of $100 for white teachers.[252]

With the opening of the Blue and Yellow Mine Banks north of Catoctin Furnace, a population shift created the need for another school. In 1897, the Board of School Commissioners bought one acre of land on the east side of the Frederick–Emmitsburg Turnpike and built Blue Mountain School #8.[253]

Many of the older generation working at the furnace were illiterate. Some were of foreign birth, and others, because of extreme poverty or a migratory life in search of work, had little opportunity for education. A typical desire for a better life for their children motivated these people to see that the next generation took advantage of educational opportunities whenever possible.[254] The one- and two-room schools of the Catoctin Furnace School District provided the means for several generations to move from illiteracy into the mainstream of society.

Chapter 8
RELIGION

Religion provided a guiding and comforting spirit to the people of the Catoctin area from the time of earliest settlement. At times, services were provided in spite of severe hardship. Those ministering to the region were devoted servants.

The early settlers of the Monoquice (Monocacy) area were largely of German origin and predominantly Lutheran. Though widely scattered, they were able on occasion to worship together. After a few years of holding services in the open or in a hayloft, they built a simple log church. The exact location of this building is not known, but it served the Monocacy region, including the pioneers along Little Hunting Creek.

One of the requirements for naturalization of German settlers was a written certification from a Protestant minister stating that the individual had received the Holy Communion. In 1743, "John Vertrees of Monoquice...received the Holy Communion of the Lord's Supper on the 26th day of June...in the Lutheran Church of Monoquice...David Chandler, Lutheran Minister." Pastor Chandler also certified that "Valentine Verdris...Martin Wezler of Monoquice...received the Holy Communion of the Lord's Supper on the 25th day of September, 1743, in the Lutheran Church of Monoquice."[255] These settlers kept their interest in the church at Monoquice, and the Vertrees were among the contributors to the purchase of the first church book in 1746.[256] However, the Moravian congregation that centered on the Graceham area attracted some members of the same families, and Moravian clergymen ministered to the people of Catoctin Furnace for many years.

The furnace and its component buildings not only served as a working area but also had social uses. On July 23, 1786, the marriage of Richard Clark and Margaret Annas was performed at Johnson Furnace by a Lutheran pastor.[257] The furnace served as a point of identification perhaps even before it was put into blast. On January 30, 1776, William Welch and Elizabeth Chedwell were married. Both lived in "the Turckey near Johnson Furnace in Frederick County."[258] Even though the furnace was leased in 1808, the ironmaster's name was used to identify the location. On October 6, 1808, when Richard Campbell married Barbara Zimmerman, the ceremony was performed at "Mr. Blackford's furnace in the presence of several people."[259] Richard and Barbara Campbell were the parents of J.F. Campbell, who later described his delight in running around the office and furnace buildings.[260]

The earliest owners of Catoctin Furnace, the Johnsons, were members of the Anglican or Episcopal Church. Baker Johnson was a vestryman of All Saints Church in Frederick in 1811, the year of his death, having served in that capacity for a number of years.[261] Several years after his death, one of his daughters, Julianna, married the Reverend John Johns, rector of All Saints. Benjamin Blackford was also described as being a staunch Episcopalian and very active in the Shenandoah Valley of Virginia.[262]

Clergymen of the Moravian Church spent a great deal of time ministering in the area of the furnace. On July 30, 1799, Brother John Frederick Schlegel talked with James Johnson and his brother(s) and sons at the furnace site. He was particularly descriptive of the scene that followed when he "visited the poor Negroes…whose inward and outward conditions are troubled." Standing around the opening of the furnace, "I depicted the Saviour as He redeemed them from sins through His suffering and death upon the cross and told how so many of their countrymen in the West Indies, through belief in the Saviour, have achieved bliss [happiness] through His death." They (the blacks present) wept very much because they were bound to work very hard during the week as well as on Sunday and were seldom able to hear the Word of God. When he finished speaking to them, Schlegel said that the signal was given, and they had to return to work.[263]

During the pastorate of Carl Gottlieb Bleck, from October 1805 to May 1, 1819, the ministry to the furnace population continued. On April 23, 1808, Brother Bleck went to the furnace and "attended to a body and preached in the graveyard on the 32nd Psalm." On October 15, 1815, Bleck and another member of the Moravian congregation went "to the Furnace and baptized two children in the death of Jesus."[264]

John Brien was a member of All Saints and was serving as a vestryman when he bought Catoctin Furnace in 1820, having been elected on April 7, 1817. He served on several committees that were appointed to contract for church building improvements and superintended some of the work. The year before his term expired in April 1822, John Brien was on the committee that was responsible for repairing the wall around the graveyard and for rough casting the walls of the church. He does not appear to have been quite so involved at All Saints after he became fully tied up in the operation of Catoctin Furnace.[265]

In 1827, Moravian pastor Samuel Reinke greatly expanded the ministry at the furnace. He held several funerals, some attended by blacks and whites. In May, he was called to the deathbed of a woman. The road was pitch dark and stony, through forested areas. Brother Reinke said that he was relieved to arrive at the home of the patient and arranged to stay overnight.[266] On July 29, 1827, Reinke held a memorial service for a man who had died several weeks before. Many people, both blacks and whites, attended. Quite a few were from the Catoctin Ironworks, where no divine services were held. Reinke described his congregation as quiet and attentive. After the service, he talked with the people, some of whom were gray-haired blacks.[267]

By September 1827, Reinke had made arrangements to hold regular services at Catoctin Furnace. He preached his first sermon on September 16, 1827, in a little schoolhouse. The crowd, made up of "all levels of people," was attentive. At the end of the year, Brother Reinke commented that he had begun preaching in English every other Sunday at the furnace, chiefly for the sake of the employees, the majority of whom were blacks.[268]

John Brien's son, Robert Coleman Brien, married Ann Elizabeth Tiernan, daughter of Luke Tiernan, a prominent Baltimore commission merchant and his wife, Nancy (Owen) of Washington County, Maryland. The Tiernans were Roman Catholics.[269] The young couple lived at Auburn with John Brien following the death of his wife, Harriet. Ann Elizabeth Brien arranged to have Roman Catholic services at Auburn and borrowed the necessary articles for Mass from Father McGarry of Mount St. Mary's, Emmitsburg.[270] A small chapel was started on the grounds of Auburn to be used for Roman Catholic services. Ann Elizabeth Brien wrote to Father McGarry on July 30, 1828, indicating that she wanted him to send "articles" for Mass to be held the following day and on Sunday. Father John J. Chanche was to be the celebrant.[271] Due to the death of Ann Brien, the little chapel was never completed, and the only other Roman Catholic service held, as listed in the Catholic Almanac, was in 1834 at Brien's Furnace.[272]

The year 1828 brought an important addition to the religious life of Catoctin Furnace. Brother Reinke continued his services, and in spite of very bad weather, about fifty were present on Sunday afternoon, January 6, the Feast of the Epiphany. By the middle of February, a "new roomy stone meeting house," which John Brien had built, was complete enough that it could be used. On Saturday evening, February 16, 1828, an independent seventy-two-year-old preacher named Hurley held the first service in the new building. The following day, Sunday, February 17, Brother Reinke preached to a crowd of one hundred persons. In commemoration of this first service, he handed out about fifty "tracts," which were received with "visible joy and gratitude. God grant that the richly scattered seed might bring in just as much ripe fruit."[273]

Brother Reinke had many interesting experiences during his years of ministry to the people of Catoctin Furnace. In March 1828, he held the funeral of an Irishman who "lived alone in a miserable hut, but through industry and thrift had accumulated $600. The man's Catholic countrymen would not go into the building (for the funeral) which was lamentable, and even at the grave most stood at a distance."[274]

On February 8, 1829, the weather was very bad. A member of the Moravian congregation and some children accompanied Reinke to Catoctin Furnace. There were only a few people, so the service was very brief, consisting of one hymn, a Bible reading and brief talk on the meaning of the reading. That same year, John Brien asked Reinke to change the time of the service to Sunday morning. However, after discussing it with his council, the idea was voted down. The German-language service was held at Graceham on Sunday mornings.[275]

By November 1831, Brother Reinke and his council had decided that more English-language services were needed at Graceham for the young people and for the English-speaking parishioners. Holding these services meant that it would be necessary to give up having services at Catoctin Furnace, which brought the minister about thirty to forty dollars per year. The council voted to increase Reinke's salary by thirty dollars a year to compensate.[276]

Services at the furnace were not stopped until the following year. On November 18, 1832, Reinke preached for the last time at Catoctin, explaining that the attendance had not been good for some time. From that time on, only special services such as baptisms, marriages and funerals were held by the Moravian minister.

On Friday, October 25, 1833, the little stone chapel that had been built by John Brien was "consecrated to the service of God by the Rt. Rev. William

Murray Stone," Episcopal bishop of Maryland.[277] It was given the name Harriet Chapel, a memorial to Brien's wife. Brother Reinke was asked to attend and lead the singing. He noted in his account of the consecration that "indeed I had been preaching there for four years."[278] He also said that the bishop's sermon was on Second Chronicles, 15:2. Afterward, the party dined with John Brien at Auburn.

As a mission of All Saints, Frederick, Harriet Chapel was supplied by visiting clergymen for a number of years. By 1850, conditions had deteriorated. Harriet A. McPherson, wife of Dr. William S. McPherson, wrote to Bishop William R. Whittingham on February 25, 1850, voicing concern and noting a need to revitalize the church. This may be the same trend that Brother Reinke had noticed in 1832 when he stated that the congregations were getting smaller. The bishop encouraged Mrs. McPherson, suggesting that occasional services could be provided at first, which would have the effect of introducing the church to the people. He also brought up the idea of a school to help provide maintenance for a clergyman.[279] In 1851, Peregrine Fitzhugh, his partner Michael M. Ege, Dr. W.S. McPherson, William Johnson and Freeman Traver, founder for Fitzhugh, notified the Vestry of All Saints that they lived at too great a distance to attend services in Frederick and wanted to organize a separate congregation within the parish so that they might "build a church at or near Catoctin Furnace."[280] All Saints Vestry consented to the application.

Photograph of Harriet Chapel, circa 1900, with stone churchyard fence and rectory to the rear left. *Photograph courtesy of the Catoctin Furnace Historical Society.*

The expanded chancel of Harriet Chapel, circa 1924. The stone arches were constructed from the stones of the dissembled Deborah furnace casting shed. *Photograph courtesy of the Catoctin Furnace Historical Society.*

In the summer of 1852, a deacon, Henry John Windsor, received a call from "the new congregation at Catoctin Furnace, a large population without any religious services." The bishop was in England, so Windsor took the initiative to move to Catoctin to begin serving the congregation.[281] Harriet McPherson was able to get some church furniture, including an altar and lectern, from St. Luke's Church in Baltimore. In a letter to John Green Proud, she shared her enthusiasm for happenings under the leadership of Henry Windsor. The chancel was to be enlarged to nineteen by eight feet, a bishop's chair was ordered and other improvements were planned. She asked what substance could be mixed with whitewash to make an appropriate color for a church, stating that they planned to "wash" the stone building outside as well as inside.[282] Windsor wrote to the bishop early in 1853, noting that he was ill and asking the bishop to arrange for his ordination as priest because of the "urgent necessity for the administration of the Holy Communion in this place."[283] Less than two weeks later, Fitzhugh and Ege sent a telegram to the bishop stating that the Reverend Mr. Windsor had died.[284]

James A. Harrell, another deacon, moved to Catoctin. He too found that not having priests' orders was a definite "impediment to success." His people had "not had the privilege of communion for twelve months," and he had been "recently called on to administer the Holy Sacrament to dying persons without the power to comply."[285] Harrell was ordained, and in May 1853, he sent a glowing report to the convention. He had baptized nineteen, the services were crowded and there was a flourishing Sunday school with twelve teachers and eighty scholars. A "liberal churchman," Peregrine Fitzhugh, had given the church a "neat and comfortable dwelling for a rectory and several acres of land for a glebe...adjoining the church."[286] There were problems, however, for in March 1854, Harrell found it necessary to write to the Missionary Society for Diocesan Missions, saying that it was "impossible for me to discharge my duties faithfully and efficiently without the services of a good horse." He was granted fifty dollars.[287]

In order to organize a new parish out of part of the territory of All Saints, application was made to the Diocesan Convention of 1855, and the boundaries of Catoctin Parish were approved.[288] Disaster struck Catoctin Parish on February 13, 1856, when the rectory caught fire. The rectory family was safe, but most of their belongings were damaged. The Harrells moved in with Peregrine Fitzhugh, but the task of rebuilding the rectory seemed to be beyond the resources of the little congregation. Two months later, James Harrell resigned as priest of Catoctin Parish.[289]

Some thought was given to merging Catoctin Parish with Ascension Parish in Westminster. The enlarged parish would have employed three priests, but this plan was dropped. The Reverend Charles M. Parkman planned to come to Catoctin Furnace as of November 1, 1856. He was interested in buying land[290] from Peregrine Fitzhugh to open a mission house, home for candidates for Holy Orders, a library and a school.[291] This plan immediately fell through because Mrs. Sophia Fitzhugh had transferred the property to another son.[292] Parkman also discovered that the vestry had no resources to finish fixing up the rectory and in fact had barely been able to close in the roof. The Reverend James G. Jacocks did accept a call to Catoctin Parish but regretted it immediately. Within days, he sent the bishop a letter saying things were "so different from what was anticipated" that he was going south.[293] He stayed on but continued to regret his decision because after five months of service, he had received only $20. He was serving four churches, scattered from Liberty to Catoctin Furnace. The bishop sent him $100, but further efforts to raise money were to no avail, so James Jacocks resigned, effective December 1, 1857.[294] Catoctin Parish still owed him $50.[295] Some of the problems of the parish may have been due to evangelistic activity that was attracting new converts. Dr. McPherson's man Harry "lost" August 25 to August 28, 1856, to attend "camp meeting."[296]

The Reverend Alfred A. Curtis served Catoctin Parish for a short time early in 1860. He considered his stay temporary as he wanted to locate closer to his widowed mother and sisters. Curtis wrote glowingly of the Easter services:

> *The church was well filled in the morning and at night it was thoroughly packed and even after much more crowding than was consistent with comfort some were unable to find seats…All our evening Lenten services were very well attended. From forty to fifty nightly assembled for the service and lectures during Passion Week…two…made their first Communion Easter Day.*[297]

Mrs. M.Z. Dorsey, a widow with a family, kept house for Curtis and remained in the rectory after he left. She was practically destitute. In 1861, she wrote to the bishop that "the times are so terrible." There were few services at Catoctin. One priest indicated that he would be willing to move to the parish without salary, in which case Mrs. Dorsey feared she and her "helpless girls" would be homeless. "Rev. Father," she wrote, "do you know of any place where we may find a home?...My eldest daughter speaks French and is a good musician, has a rare voice for church music."[298] The family stayed in the area because "since the arrival of Miss Dorsey our services have been rendered much more attractive by the addition of music," wrote J. Taylor Chambers, a young deacon assigned to Catoctin Parish in May 1864.[299] Chambers felt the need, as had earlier deacons, to be ordained to the priesthood in order to carry out the ministry of the parish. In September 1865, after having served at Catoctin Furnace for sixteen months, Chambers wrote that he had doubts that the church would maintain a rector. The receipts during these months had been less than $200. He had been given $150 and his board during the first year, but since the people of the parish were "few and poor," he was beginning to despair of continuing his post. He felt that no parish in the diocese was so needy. Repairs were needed on the church, and during the summer Chambers had collected $40 toward them, calling himself "a beggar."[300]

The Reverend Robert Clarkson, brother-in-law of Harriet A. McPherson, visited at Auburn for Christmas 1868. There was no priest at Harriet Chapel, so Clarkson held Christmas services, and with Bishop Whittingham's permission, administered the Holy Rite of Confirmation to a group that included Dr. McPherson; Mary McPherson, his daughter; Elizabeth, daughter of John Kunkel; and Amanda Ott, daughter of George Ott, Kunkel's manager.[301]

The Reverend Thomas O. Tongue moved to Catoctin Furnace on July 18, 1869. He found things "in bad condition. Owing to the want of a clergyman, the people had strayed to a 'meeting' nearby…the Sunday School had dwindled to a shadow and Catoctin had only five communicants."[302] Tongue received $96 per year for operating the post office, and "Dr. McPherson and Mr. Kunkel each gave $100, the…offertory $100 more." He described the house as "comfortable" and said the church could be "enclosed and repaired for but little."[303]

The following year, 1871, James B. Avirett, a deacon, moved to Catoctin with his family.[304] He worked hard, serving four churches and planning a chapel in Mechanicstown, which he proposed to name Whittingham Chapel in honor of the bishop.[305] In the first week of February 1872, fire again struck Catoctin rectory. Afterward, Avirett wrote that the people were "doing all in their power to put a roof over [us]."[306] Avirett was also feeling pressure from the words of a "vagrant Methodist preacher about the Episcopal Church's work among the rich and its neglect of the poor."[307] He hoped the excitement would wear off, but the stresses of the parish proved too great, and in August, Avirett, too, left Catoctin.[308]

The Methodists did meet with enough success in the area to be able to lay the cornerstone for their Catoctin Methodist Church[309] in 1877. The frame building was heated by a coal stove. During a revival, one of the faithful became so excited "getting religion" that he grabbed the hot stovepipe in his hands.[310] Revivals and preaching services were also held from time to time in the "meeting house." These occasions were highly charged with emotion as some in the group shouted and climbed over the seats.[311] Later, converts were dipped (baptized) in Locust Pond, which had at one time been part of the furnace operation.[312] Early doubts about the effect of the Methodists on the village people did not keep them from attending both churches. It was standard procedure to go from church to church on Sunday.[313]

The year 1889 brought a new disaster to Catoctin Furnace. Little Hunting Creek overflowed its banks during the same late May storm that triggered the Johnstown Flood. The first floor of the rectory was flooded, forcing the rector, the Reverend Richard Whittingham, to retreat to the second floor. During the summer, the parishioners were again called on to help repair the building.[314]

This was a time of economic uncertainty at the furnace. Operational changes made work spasmodic. Some of the men went to work for the Western Maryland Railroad, and as a result, the worst tragedy in the history of the village occurred in June 1905. A fast train crashed into a work train

Photograph of the Ransom train wreck, June 17, 1905. *Photograph courtesy of the Catoctin Furnace Historical Society.*

carrying many men from Catoctin Furnace. When the train carrying the bodies of those killed pulled into Mechanicstown, there was hardly a family from Catoctin that had not lost a member. The rector at that time was the Reverend Ernest McGill, Dr. McPherson's son-in-law. It was a time of tragedy for the village.

During the years that the Catoctin Furnace iron complex operated, the people were served by a number of religious denominations, all of which are still flourishing in the general area. Religion furnished solace in times of trouble, strength when it was needed and the joy of sharing with friends and neighbors.

Chapter 9
THREATENED DESTRUCTION AND PRESERVATION

The transformation of the Catoctin iron complex from abandoned ruins into a touchstone for national cultural memory took place over the course of the twentieth century, a century marked by triumph, tragedy, success, failure, determination, perseverance and luck and culminating in the village of today. The final shutdown of the furnace at Catoctin in 1903 had a devastating effect on the people of the village. Many were forced to leave to find employment. A sizeable number went to work for the Western Maryland Railroad, a fact that led to the greatest single tragedy to befall the people of the northern part of Frederick County. On Saturday, June 17, 1905, seven men from the Catoctin Furnace area were killed when the train they were riding home collided head-on with a second train near Ransom Station, outside Baltimore. Seven of the injured were also from the area. No one was untouched by the tragedy, which left a number of widows and fatherless children and dominated the thinking in the village of Catoctin Furnace for years.

A stave mill, operated by Oscar H. Trexler and G.J. Heintzleman, trading as Hickory Run Manufacturing Company of Allentown, Pennsylvania, moved into Catoctin Furnace following shutdown of the Blue Mountain mines. The mill operated from 1914 until the early 1920s, under a contract made with Joseph Thropp, which allowed removal of timber from Catoctin Furnace lands. Millions of barrel staves were sawed and shipped by rail from Catoctin. A number of jobs were provided by this industry, not only in the mill, but also in the mountains cutting timber.

The storage yard of the Hickory Run Manufacturing Company at Catoctin Furnace, circa 1910, filled with chestnut and oak lumber for the manufacturing of barrel staves. *Photograph courtesy of Mary Rae Cantwell.*

Joseph E. Thropp, the man responsible for the end of the Catoctin iron complex, went bankrupt in 1923. In that year, he sold the majority of his holdings in Catoctin to Lancelot Jacques, a descendant of Thomas Johnson's partner, and Stanley Hauver.[315] Included in the purchase were the village houses, the remains of the furnace complex, the ironmaster's mansion and at least 6,242 acres, out of Thropp's 10,000 acres.[316] Jacques and Hauver gave the residents of the village the opportunity to buy their houses, which most of them did at prices ranging from $250 to $450. Jacques took a special interest in the mansion house, reportedly intending to occupy it himself and then changing his mind and attempting to sell it for a large profit.

Shortly after purchasing the furnace property, Messrs. Jacques and Hauver gave Catoctin Parish an old stone casting house that stood in the midst of the furnace complex. The casting house was torn down and the stones moved across the highway to Harriet Chapel. William McPherson McGill used the stones to construct a new chancel separated from the nave by three Gothic arches. In addition, a large room was built behind the chancel.

In 1926, Jacques sold a tract to the Potomac Hills Development Company;[317] in 1929, another tract was sold to Lawrence Richey, executive secretary to President Hoover, who used the grounds for occasional camping;[318] and in 1937, another tract was sold to E.A. Nicodemus.[319] Nicodemus deeded his property to the federal government the following year.[320] This acquisition was part of a broader strategy by the National Park Service to obtain thousands of acres in the Catoctin Mountains and transform them into recreational demonstration projects, creating a buffer zone for the presidential retreat of Camp David in the process. In 1952, Conrad Wirth, the director of the National Park Service, initiated the process of transferring the southern area of the Catoctin Recreational Demonstration Area to the State of Maryland. In June 1954, Maryland governor McKeldin received the title of 4,446.879 acres for inclusion in the Maryland State Park System.[321] Cunningham Falls State Park was created out of this agreement.

Concerns for the built heritage of the Catoctin area were raised on the national level as early as 1936, when the National Park Service acquired the grounds. At this time, the manor house, the Isabella stack and a retaining wall were the most predominant features still standing, but historians were also interested in the archaeological features. An early attempt at archaeological investigation was thwarted that same year when the excavation supervisor, who was not an archaeologist by profession, was ordered to stop work immediately. Archaeological investigations on the site did not resume until many years later.

Photograph of the dilapidated Ironmaster's House circa the 1950s. From the Clement S. Brinton Collection. *Photograph courtesy of Eleutherian Mills Historical Library, Greenville, Delaware.*

A decade later, Frederick residents began to express concerns about the conditions of the manor house of Catoctin. The boxwoods surrounding the house were removed and replanted at the White House. The race pond where Roosevelt fished was destroyed during the construction of Route 15. By the 1940s, it was falling into ruin. Individuals conferred with Congressman J. Glenn Beall and National Park Service officials to urge restoration of the Catoctin House. However, no funds were available at the time, and the ruin and decay of the manor house was allowed to continue. However, the beauty and historic character of the village continued to be evident. On October 30, 1932, famed Baltimore photographer A. Aubrey Bodine visited Catoctin Furnace and photographed the homes with their picket fences lining the gravel road. He returned at least twice in 1949 and 1965. A photograph of the double log house, later the headquarters of the Catoctin Furnace Historical Society, Inc., appeared in the June 13, 1965 issue of the *Baltimore Sun*.

After decades of neglect, the structures associated with the Catoctin ironwork complex began to receive the attention they deserved in the 1950s with the approaching threat of transportation development. Originally part of the Thurmont and Emmitsburg Turnpike, the road eventually designated U.S. Route 15 was purchased and paved by the Maryland State Roads Commission between 1911 and 1915. This sealed underneath the road numerous archaeological features. North of Catoctin Furnace, the Thurmont Bypass was completed in 1958 to Owens Creek, but the original U.S. Route 15 continued to run through the village of Catoctin Furnace.

Concerns about the road-building activity were raised as early as 1955, when the Historical Society of Frederick County informed the State Roads Commission that they would oppose any route endangering the manor house or the old Catoctin Furnace.[322] The secretary of the interior also weighed in, informing the governor of Maryland that the relocation of U.S. 15 through the eastern part of the park would be a violation of the deed conveyed by the Department of the Interior to the State of Maryland.[323]

In the years that followed the road-building activity near Catoctin Furnace, newspapers and magazine articles showed renewed interest:

> *The rounds that followed the "shot heard 'round the world" may well have been smelted right here in Frederick County…but the furnaces which did the job are crumbling from the weight of time and neglect.*[324]

Some of the most important activity took place over the course of the early 1970s when the Maryland State Highway Administration proposed the creation of two additional lanes for U.S. Route 15. The existing two-lane highway, completed in 1962 and located between the mountain and the village, was unsafe and responsible for a high number of accidents and fatalities, and thus the expansion was promoted with a sense of urgency by local and state government alike. A series of public hearings was held to discuss the proposed improvements, with a number of local residents concerned for the impact on the historical and archaeological resources in the Catoctin ironworking complex. The original proposal called for the widening of a twenty-mile stretch of the road from Frederick to the northern Maryland border. The seventy-six-foot wide median and the second set of lanes would have eliminated two mine pits associated with the complex and would have come within fifty feet of the old ironworks.[325] Frank Mentzer, superintendent of Catoctin Mountain Park, raised concerns that the vibrations from traffic would threaten the old furnaces.[326]

The passage of the Historic Preservation Act of 1966, which directed agencies to consider the effect of their undertaking, such as the proposed U.S. Route 15 project, on historic and cultural resources, resulted in several archaeological investigations. Contract Archaeology, Inc. was hired to conduct investigations into the impact of the dualization on recorded and unrecorded historical landmarks and archaeology. The study, published in 1971, recommended an alternative to the proposed route that would minimize the destruction of historic and archaeological features.

The publicity surrounding these events initiated a process that ended in the listing of the Catoctin Furnace Historic District, including 119.6 acres, twelve buildings and three structures, on the National Register of Historic Places in February 1972. Other properties were added later. At the same time, Frank Mentzer published a series of sixteen articles in a local newspaper to inform the public of the interesting history and importance of the Catoctin Furnace and garner support for preserving the site.[327] On the federal level, the National Park Service formally invoked protection for the Catoctin Furnace Historic District under the National Historic Preservation Act of 1966.[328] The National Park Service offered to meet with representatives from several federal and state agencies in order to seek a resolution to the matter.

The United States Department of the Interior again weighed in on the situation, stating that the proposed dualization would destroy the environmental setting and historical integrity of Catoctin Furnace, and that the only viable alternative would be moving the dualization to the east, a suggestion also made by locals a year earlier.[329]

The Maryland State Highway Administration was required to modify the path of U.S. Route 15, and more archaeological survey work was undertaken from 1977 to 1980 to understand the effects of the disturbance on the local archaeological resources. Kenneth and Ronald Orr determined through their investigations that only two out of ninety-two impacted features would be destroyed by the road construction, and therefore the alignment in question could proceed after mitigation work was conducted.[330] In 1980, a plan was established by several parties and the State Highway Administration that included intensive archaeological investigations before construction of the highway, measurements taken during and after construction to mitigate and measure noise, vibrations and pollution and the construction of a pedestrian overpass connecting the Catoctin Furnace area with the parklands west of the highway. The mitigation plan included, besides archaeological excavation, research on the land records and oral history. Retaining walls were constructed for the furnace area during the construction of the second lane to protect the ore pits and the race pond. The expanded U.S. Route 15 north of Frederick was completed by 1985. Over the course of a decade, the Maryland State Highway Administration had stirred up an unanticipated and inadvertent flurry of interest and activity in these old ruins along the highway.

Amongst this renewed fervor for the history of the site and its preservation, especially in preparation for the nation's bicentennial celebration in 1976, the Catoctin Furnace Historical Society, Inc., was formed in 1973 by G. Eugene Anderson with Clement E. Gardiner, J. Franklin Mentzer and Earl M. Shankle as the four incorporators. The society was primarily meant to "foster and promote the restoration of the Catoctin Furnace Historic District…and to maintain the same…exclusively for educational and scientific purposes…to acquire and maintain the old country store and dwellings in the community…to exhibit to coming generations our heritage of the past."[331] Two years later, they proposed the formation of an advisory committee to assist and advise the Department of Natural Resources in the historic preservation and restoration of the Catoctin Furnace National Historic Site within Cunningham Falls State Park. The Department of Natural Resources was receptive, and a committee of nine members was formed to this end, which would influence the Catoctin Furnace and Manor Area Master Plan adopted in 1983.[332]

Despite the enthusiasm exhibited by the local Catoctin Furnace Historical Society during the early 1970s, it took some work to garner appropriate funds and wider support from the local community. The historical society turned to foundations affiliated with the steel industry for funding options, but to no avail.[333] The state budget contributed $26,000 for the stabilization of the furnace walls in 1973, but this was not enough to complete the job.[334] After a public meeting in Thurmont, where the issue of the furnace preservation was brought up, Robert Bushnell of the Department of Natural Resources remarked that "frankly, there wasn't a whole lot of support from the people there."[335] G. Eugene Anderson, president of the Catoctin Furnace Historical Society, Inc., and his wife, Elizabeth Y. Anderson, intent on gaining support in the local community, bought one of the circa 1774 stone worker cottages in the village and began the expensive process of restoring it to a pre–Civil War likeness. It was hoped that this would encourage the preservation and restoration of other workers' houses, making these living public exhibits of the industrial heritage of the site.[336] Restoration and renovation of other worker cottages followed.

In 1977, the double log house was acquired by the Catoctin Furnace Historical Society, Inc. in two purchases. The northern section was purchased for $3,000 from Donald and Pauline Miller, and the southern (larger) section was purchased from Franklin and Louise Fraley for $6,000.

Original 1774 stone workers house as restored by G. Eugene and Elizabeth Yourtee Anderson, currently owned by Jerry and Nancy Anderson. *Photograph courtesy of the Catoctin Furnace Historical Society, by Donald Frame.*

Circa 1810 double log collier's house, during restoration by (and headquarters of) the Catoctin Furnace Historical Society. *Photograph courtesy of Joel T. Anderson.*

Some efforts paid off. In 1975, the casting shed at the Catoctin Furnace was rebuilt. A short archaeological study was conducted on the site to save information that would be disturbed by the reconstruction.[337] This project made use of information provided by William Renner, a local resident who was able to produce sketch maps of the structures in the complex from memory and oral tradition. In the following decade, a number of archaeological studies were conducted at the Catoctin Furnace area to gain a better understanding of the overall quality of the archaeology and standing buildings and to establish management and planning guidelines.[338] These would help shape the planning implemented by the Maryland Department of Natural Resources. The archaeological reports contributed not only to the academic knowledge but also to the sense of the national historical importance of the site within the local context.

Work in the complex continued and expanded throughout the 1980s. In 1981, work began to stabilize the ruins of the ironmaster's house. A three-phase plan was implemented in 1984 to construct a visitors' center and interpretative trail for the Catoctin Furnace. After the stabilization of the Isabella stack and the ironmaster's house, a trail was constructed that included the pedestrian bridge over U.S. Route 15 and a paved parking lot was added. The collier's log house, which was acquired by the Catoctin Furnace Historical Society, Inc., in 1977, was restored over the course of a few years with private monies and a grant from the Maryland Historical Trust.[339] Mr. Robert M. Gardiner, a descendant of the longtime owners of Auburn Farm, donated the majority of the funds as a memorial to his aunt, Miss Louise McPherson.

The sesquicentennial anniversary of Harriet Chapel in 1983 was a cause of great celebration and commemoration in the village of Catoctin Furnace. On Sunday, October 30, 1983, the Right Reverend William J. Cox celebrated the sesquicentennial Eucharist in the style of 1833. A history of Harriet Chapel, *Faith in the Furnace, A History of Harriet Chapel, Catoctin Furnace, Maryland*, was written by Elizabeth Y. Anderson and enthusiastically received, as was a second manuscript, *Them Was the Good Days of Eatin'*, an oral history of traditional village foodways.

Interest has not waned in the Catoctin Iron Furnace even one hundred years after it was closed down. In October 2004, the park initiated a "Spirits of the Furnace" guided night hike, meant to entertain but also to educate the public on the history of the site.[340] The Catoctin Furnace Historical Society, Inc., continues its work to share the rich heritage of the site and involve the local, living descendants in the presentation of its history. Annual events such as "Spring in the Village" and "Traditional Village Christmas" bring visitors to Catoctin Furnace and give residents the opportunity to share their rich heritage. The village retains its eighteenth- and nineteenth-century feel, and the visitor to the collier's log house can experience firsthand the lifestyle of a furnace worker. The reincarnation of this complex evokes the concern of people on local, state and national levels in the preservation of their history.

NOTES

Chapter 1

1. Maryland Land Patent EI#6:136.
2. A swampy area where there was a natural salt deposit. According to Dr. Grace Tracey, this patent was located just west of Little Hunting Creek—land that was later to become part of "Auburn." Tracey, *Notes from the Records of Old Monocacy*, 92.
3. "Turckey" was used as part of the names of many patents, probably because of the plentiful numbers of wild turkeys nearby.
4. Strassberger, *Pennsylvania German Pioneers*, 51.
5. Maryland Land Patent LG#B:577.
6. Will of John Vertrees. Original Will #1:55, January 27, 1753.
7. "Plat of Old Forge" *BGF* 3:312. John Milner Associates report fixing date of construction and use of forge.
8. Andrews, *History of* Maryland, 216.
9. Ibid., 217.
10. Robbins. *Maryland's Iron Industry*, 20.
11. Maryland Land Patent BC&GS 27:215, the future site of the furnace at Catoctin.
12. Maryland Land Patent BC&GS 22:452.
13. State of Maryland Board of Natural Resources, James T. Singewald.
14. Limestone is needed for flux in the iron furnace.
15. Located in present-day Washington County, Maryland.
16. Maryland Land Patent BC&GS 42:3–8.
17. Will of John Vertrees. Frederick County Land Record M:147.

18. Maryland Land Patent BC&GS 42:3–8.

19. Mentzer. "Spirit of Catoctin.".

20. Letter from James Johnson Jr. to his children. The house referred to may have been Wayside on Auburn property or another house later demolished.

21. Frederick County Land Record WR 24:436.

22. Frederick County Land Record WR 24:435–36. Construction at Green Spring Furnace took about eighteen months. Assuming that conditions at Catoctin were similar, it would have been mid-1776 when the furnace first went into blast. This reasoning is confirmed by 1776 correspondence, which follows.

23. Western Maryland.

24. Delaplaine, *Life of Thomas Johnson*, 142.

25. Williams. *History of Frederick County*, 95.

26. Revolutionary War Papers Series A, 6636/4/42 Archives of Maryland.

27. If Catoctin was not yet in blast, these may have been cast at Green Spring or at Hampton.

28. *Journal & Correspondence of the Maryland Council of Safety*, July 7–December 31, 1776, 92.

29. Revolutionary War Papers Series A, 6636/4/72. There is no evidence now available that Catoctin was ever successful in casting cannon. The foremost cannon maker in this area appears to have been Samuel Hughes of Antietam, later of Principio (Cecil Furnace).

30. *Dunlap's Maryland Journal and Baltimore Advertiser* 3, no. 120.

31. Fire back: a large iron plate placed at the back of a fireplace for fire protection and to reflect heat forward.

32. Record Group 93—M 859, Roll 103, Document #29632.

33. Ibid., Document #29633.

34. Refers to the Battle of Yorktown.

35. Record Group 93—M 859, Roll 103, Document #29634.

36. Ibid., Document #29631.

37. M247, Roll 197, item 41, vol. 4, 477–78.

38. Ibid., 485–87.

39. Ibid., 482–83.

40. Revolutionary Records. Agents Letter Book #1, 15.

41. Record Group 93, Roll 73, Frame 311, #21821.

42. Circa 1790. Reed, *Cultural Analysis*.

43. His large manor house south of Catoctin.

44. Letter from James Johnson Jr., Frederick County Historical Society.

45. Frederick County Deed WR 8:286.

46. See Chapter 5: "The Black Population."

47. Lesley, *Iron Manufacturer's Guide*, 50.

48. Lower Frederick County, *Frederick Town Herald* 9, no. 46.

49. Holdcraft, *Names in Stone*.

50. Early spelling. Delaplaine, *Life of Thomas Johnson*, 391.

51. Berkeley Springs, West Virginia.

52. Rumsey, *A Plan*, 22.

53. Ibid.

54. Alexander, *Report on the Manufacture of Iron*, 79.

55. Frederick County Land Record WR 12:452.

56. Frederick County Assessment Record 1798.

57. Frederick County Land Record WR 24:435–36.

58. Frederick County Survey Record THO 1:224–26.

59. More on this in Chapter 6: "The Worker and His Family."

60. Letter from L. Minor Blackford to Frederick County Historical Society, October 11, 1947.

61. Bining. *Pennsylvania Iron Manufacture*.

62. *Blackford Family Bible*.

63. Frederick County Will RB1:192–200.

64. James Johnson Jr. letter.

65. Frederick County Will RB1:192–200.

66. Ibid.

67. *Frederick Town Herald*, 10, nos. 6 & 7.

68. Ibid.

Chapter 2

69. Swank, *History of the Manufacture of Iron*, 155.

70. Ibid.

71. Frederick County Land Records WR 44:723–27.

72. Ibid.

73. *Frederick Town Herald* 18, no. 45.

74. Frederick County Land Record JS 10: 10–12.

75. Ibid., 13–15.

76. Now West Virginia.

77. *Frederick Town Herald*, April 1, 1820.

78. Frederick County Land Record JS 16: 324–25.

79. Frederick County Equity Record #1399, HS 4: 189.

80. Lesley, *Iron Manufacturer's Guide*, 50.

81. Grove, *History of Carrolton Manor*, 408–09.

82. Reed, *Cultural Analysis*, 14–15.

83. See Chapter 7: "Education" and Chapter 8: "Religion."

84. Frederick County Equity Record #1399, HS 4:122–23, 213.

85. Ibid. Meredith Papers, Maryland Historical Society. Hughes letters, property of C.E. Gardiner, Catoctin Furnace, Maryland.

86. Frederick County Land Record HS15:304.

87 Equity #1399, 219.

88. Letter, Henry A. Brien to John McPherson Jr., February 2, 1835. Property of C.E. Gardiner.

89. Frederick County Land Record HS 19:213.

90. Ibid., HS 14: 121–24.

91. Ibid., HS 15: 300–09.

92. French. *History of the Rise and Progress*, 28–30.

93. Consignment Slip, B&O Archives, Museum of Transportation, Baltimore.

94. Fitzhugh, *A Fitzhugh Chart.*

95. Williams, *History of Washington County*, 200.

96. National Heritage Corp., *Report on a Historical Survey*, 12.

97. Heiges, *Henry William Stiegel*, 28, 29, 114.

98. *Examiner*, September 14, 1853.

99. Frederick County Land Record BGF 3: 312–13.

100. Williams, *History of Frederick County*, 278. McPherson Farm Book, property of C.E. Gardiner.

101. Frederick County Equity Record #2805 BGF 3:93.

102. Lesley, *Iron Manufacturer's Guide*, 50, states that furnace #2 was cold blast. Mentzer, "Fitzhugh & Partners," states that Isabella furnace was hot blast. Evidence indicates Mentzer is correct.

103. Frederick County Land Record ES7:302–03.

104. McPherson Farm Book, entry February 3, 1855.

Chapter 3

105. *Biographical Directory of the American Congress.*

106. Frederick County Equity Record #2805, BGF 3:110.

107. Frederick County Land Record BGF 1: 503–04.

108. Equity Record #2805.

109. Frederick County Land Record JWLC 4: 278–79.

110. *Examiner*, May 6, 1858

111. The importance of the desk and the missing business records became apparent during the suit between Kunkel and Fitzhugh recounted in Equity #2805.

112. Frederick County Land Record JWLC 4:278–79.

113. Frederick County Land Records JWLC 4: 278–79 and JWLC 4:159–61.

114. Plat-Equity #5229, WIP 5: 457.

115. Robbins, *Maryland's Iron Industry*, 52.

116. American Iron and Steel Association, *Directory of the Iron and Steel Works*.

117. Letters Patent 182, 371, RG 241, National Archives.

118. Frederick County Tax Assessment Book #15, 1876.

119. Singewald lists the year as 1867, 147.

120. Scharf, *History of Western Maryland*, 629.

121. *Frederick News*, Wednesday, April 18, 1888, sale advertisement.

122. Frederick County Land Record CM 2:461.

123. More in Chapter 8: "Education."

124. Richards, *Kunkel Family of Frederick*.

125. Equity Record #5229, WIP 5:401.

126. Waesche, "Economic History of Catoctin Furnace."

127. *Frederick News*, April 18, 1888; Equity Record #5529, 412–13.

128. Singewald, *Report on the Iron Ores of Maryland*, 148.

129. *Frederick News*, March 1899.

130. *Sunday Herald*, Washington, October 8, 1899; Land Record DHH 3:614.

131. Frederick County Land Record DHH 5:215–18.

132. Catoctin Mountain Iron Company Payroll Book, 1899.

133. Waesche, "Economic History of Catoctin Furnace."

134. *Baltimore Sun*, January 17, 1901.

135. Singewald, *Iron Ores of Maryland*, 148.

136. Frederick County Land Record STH284:567.

137. *Baltimore Sun*, February 20, 1906.

Chapter 4

138. Much of the knowledge contained in this chapter has been gathered through a long-term interest in Catoctin Furnace, as well as exploratory visits to both Hopewell and Cornwall, restored eighteenth-century iron furnaces in nearby areas of Pennsylvania.

139. Singewald, *Iron Ores of Maryland*, 146.

140. Lesley. *Iron Manufacturer's Guide*, 50.

141. Singewald, *Iron Ores of Maryland*, 146.

142. See Chapter Seven: "The Worker and Family Life," for further details on the making of charcoal.

143. Boyer, *Charcoal Burner*, 34.

144. "Trustee's Sale."

145. Singewald, *Iron Ores of Maryland*, 199.

146. Ibid.

147. Ibid., 198.

148. Tyson, *Second Report of the State Agricultural Chemist*, 71.

149. "An Industrious Boom?" and *Maryland., Its Resources*, 138, noted, "The Catoctin Furnace in Frederick County, formally obtained its flux from extensive limestone quarries at Cavetown, on the Western Maryland Railroad, on the opposite side of the Blue Ridge." The works had once employed three hundred woodcutters and charcoal burners and one hundred mines of brown hematite ore. Catoctin Furnace Post Office had operated from 1851 to 1854.

150. United States Patent Office, *Correspondence*.

151. Singewald, *Iron Ores of Maryland*, 147.

152. "An Industrious Boom?"

153. Walker, *Hopewell Village*, 141.

154. Williams, *History of Frederick County*, 278. Also McPherson Farm Book.

155 Singewald, *Iron Ores of Maryland*, 236.

156. Ibid.

157. Ibid.

158. Ibid., 237.

159. Grove, *History of Carrollton Manor*, 408–09.

160. Lesley, *Iron Manufacturer's Guide*, 50.

161. Ibid. Other researchers, such as Mentzer, have suggested that the Isabella stack was a hot-blast furnace.

162. American Iron and Steel Association, *Directory, 1874*, 32.

163. Ibid.

164. Waesche, "Economic History of Catoctin Furnace."

165. American Steel and Iron Association. *Directory, 1894–1896*, 29.

Chapter 5

166. Frederick County Land Record WR 8:286.

167. Diary of John Frederick Schlegel, 1799. As they were gathered at the top of the furnace, "pour" probably refers to charging of the furnace.

168. Diary of Samuel Reinke, 1827.

169. Seabold and Seabold, *Frederick County, Maryland*.

170. Crowl, *Maryland During and After the Revolution*, 139.

171. A collier worked in the mountain burning charcoal. Waggoners were experienced in handling teams of horses pulling large wagons such as were used in hauling for the furnace.

172. There are strong traditions that certain houses at Catoctin Furnace were at one time slave quarters. Interview with Mary Miller Martin, February 19, 1982.

173. Lewis. *Coal, Iron and Slaves*, 13.

174. Ibid., 82–83.

175. Census of the United States, 1820.

176. Ibid.

177. Blackford family history. Letter from Dr. L.M. Blackford to Frederick County Historical Society, October 11, 1947.

178. Blackford, *Letters from Lee's Army*, 3.

179. Frederick County Land Record JS 10:13–15.

180. Census of the United States, 1820.

181. Ibid., 1840.

182. Williams, *History of Washington County*, 247.

183. Meredith Papers, MS 1367. It is hard to document treatment of blacks, but in some cases, they may have been dealt with harshly. According to informant William Renner, one troublemaker was pushed into the stack at Catoctin.

184. Campbell, "Some Notes on Frederick County's Participation," 55–59.

185. Hitselberger and Dor, *Bridge in Time*.

186. *Convention Journal*, 1856, 69.

187. Ibid., 56.

188. Mid-Atlantic Archaeological Research, Inc., *Archaeological Data Recovery*, IV, 1–3.

189. Interview with William Renner, November 4, 1981.

Chapter 6

190. See Chapter 8: "Religion."

191. See Chapter 5: "The Black Population."

192. *Baltimore Sun*, June 4, 1845.

193. Frederick County Deed WR 8:286.

194. Diary of Samuel Reinke, 1828.

195. Frederick County Will Book GME 1:1.

196. Census of the U.S., 1860, 1870.

197. Ibid., 1870.

198. Diary of Samuel Reinke, 1826.

199. Boyer, *The Charcoal Burner*, 32–33.

200. Census of the United States, 1870.

201. Interview with Joseph Carbaugh, November 30, 1981.

202. Census of the U.S., 1870.

203. Hitselberger and Dor, *Bridge in Time*.

204. Census of the U.S., 1870.

205. Hitselberger and Dor, *Bridge in Time*.

206. Census of the U.S., 1870; *General Frederick County Directory*, 210, 274.

207. McPherson Farm Books #1 and #2.

208. Census of the U.S., 1870.

209. Interview with Lloyd Hoke, November 9, 1981.

210. Census of the U.S., 1870.

211. Ibid.

212. Ibid.; Interview with Jessie Reed Stitely, October 2, 1981.

213. *Frederick Town Herald* 10, nos. 6 & 7.

214. Catoctin Furnace ledger, 1899.

215. Interview with Clinton Miller and Margaret Anders Hoke, November 9, 1981.

216. Frederick County Bill of Sale JS 18:104.

217. Frederick County Bill of Sale JS 18:105.

218. Miller-Hoke interview. Tick: a cloth case filled with feathers, straw, etc.

219. Shuff payroll book.

220. Catoctin Furnace Historical Society 1899 Ledger.

221. McPherson Farm Book #1.

222. Ibid.

223. Interview with Mary Miller Martin, February 18, 1982.

224. Note listing Shuff personal property.

225. Frederick County Bill of Sale JS 10:13–15.

226. Interview with Joseph Carbaugh.

227. Ibid.

228. Interview with Ethel Carbaught Devilbliss, April 24, 1981.

229. Interview with Roger Penwell, January 30, 1982.

230. See Chapter 7: "Education."

Chapter 7

231. Oerter, *History of Graceham*, 24.

232. Campbell, "Autobiography of J.F. Campbell."

233. Diary of Samuel Reinke, 1827.

234. Williams, *History of Frederick County*, 226.

235. Minutes of Board of School Commissioners for Frederick County, 1839.

236. Bond, *Map of Frederick County*, 1858. Present Blacks Mill Road and Hessong Bridge.

237. Minutes of Board of School Commissioners.

238. Ibid., February 22, 1841.

239. Minutes of Board of School Commissioners. (Note: mensuration means "the branch of mathematics that deals with methods of finding length of lines, area of surfaces, and volume of solids.")
240. Minutes from the Board of School Commissioners.
241. Letter from Bishop William Rollison Whittingham to Harriet A. McPherson, March 5, 1850.
242. The "interested lady" was probably Harriet A. McPherson.
243. *Convention Journal,* May 30, 1854, 69.
244. Ibid., May 1856, 56.
245. Letter from the Reverend Charles M. Parkman to Bishop William Rollison Whittingham, September 23, 1856. Archives of Diocese of Maryland, Maryland Historical Society.
246. Frederick County Land Record CM 2:461. School located on the north side of present Kellys Store Road.
247. Minutes of the Board of School Commissioners, February 2, 1870.
248. Minutes of the Board of School Commissioners, December 31, 1869.
249. Letter from the Reverend James Averitt to Bishop Whittingham, August 19, 1872.
250. Interview with Joseph Carbaugh, November 30, 1981.
251. Interview with Jessie Reed Stitely, October 2, 1981.
252. Frederick County Board of School Commissioners Records, 1872.
253. Corner of the present Blue Mountain Road.
254. Interview with Jessie Reed Stitely, January 10, 1982.

Chapter 8

255. Provincial Court Judgments EI 7:296.
256. Cunz, *Maryland Germans,* 64.
257. *Records of Marriages and Burials in the Monocacy Church,* 48.
258. Ibid.
259. Ibid., 76.
260. Diary of J.F. Campbell; see Chapter 7: "Education."
261. All Saints Vestry Minutes, Frederick. During these years, it appears that Johnson was living in his Frederick house.
262. Blackford family history.
263. Diary of John Frederick Schlegel, 1799.
264. Diary of Carl Gottlieb Bleck, 1815. Crosschecking the register for that year, the names of these children appear to be Solomon Hancock and William Carothers. The expression "baptizing...in the death of Jesus" was not unusual.

265. All Saints Vestry Minutes.

266. Diary of Samuel Reinke, 1827.

267. Ibid.

268. Ibid.

269. Williams, *History of Frederick County*.

270. Letter from Ann Elizabeth Brien to Father McGarry, Mount St. Mary's, Emmitsburg, September 12, 1827.

271. Ibid., July 30, 1828.

272. *Catholic Almanac*, 1834; Archdiocese of Baltimore, 48. Robert Brien died in 1834. This service might have been a memorial to him.

273. Diary of Samuel Reinke, 1828.

274. Ibid. See Chapter 6: "The Worker and Family Life."

275. Diary of Samuel Reinke, 1829.

276. Ibid., 1831.

277. Journal of Convention of Diocese of Maryland, 1834, 35; Diary of Samuel Reinke, 1833.

278. Reinke diary, 1833.

279. Letter from Bishop William Rollison Whittingham to Mrs. Harriet A. McPherson, March 5, 1850.

280. Petition to the Convention of the Diocese of Maryland, 1851.

281. Letter from Henry John Windsor to Bishop Whittingham, September 28, 1852.

282. Letter from Harriet A. McPherson to John Green Proud. MS 1530.

283. Letter from Henry Windsor to Bishop Whittingham, January 5, 1853.

284. Telegram from Fitzhugh & Ege to Bishop Whittingham, January 18, 1853.

285. Letter from James A. Harrell to Bishop Whittingham, October 24, 1853.

286. Convention of Journal, 1854, 70, 71; Frederick County Land Record ES 7:302-303. Seven and a half acres of land "for the use of the Protestant Episcopal Church...and for no other purpose whatsoever."

287. Letter from James A. Harrell to Bishop Whittingham, March 21, 1854.

288. Act for the Establishment of Catoctin Parish.

289. Letter from James A. Harrell to Bishop Whittingham, April 18, 1856.

290. Windy Hill Farm.

291. Letter from the Reverend Charles M. Parkman to Bishop Whittingham, August 29, 1856.

292. Ibid., September 23, 1856.

293. Letter from James G. Jacocks to Bishop Whittingham, December 23, 1856.

294. Ibid., December 14, 1857.

295. Ibid., June 4, 1858.

296. McPherson Farm Book #1, week ending August 30, 1856.

297. Letter from the Reverend Alfred A. Curtis to Bishop Whittingham, April 9, 1860. Father Curtis became a Roman Catholic priest and later a bishop.

298. Letter from Mary C. Dorsey to Bishop Whittingham. September 30, 1861.

299. Letter from J. Taylor Chambers to Bishop Whittingham, May 29, 1865.

300 Letter from J. Taylor Chambers to Bishop Whittingham, September 22, 1865.

301. Letter from Robert H. Clarkson to Bishop Whittingham, January 1, 1869.

302. Letter from Thomas O. Tongue to Bishop Whittingham, November 3, 1869.

303. Ibid., March 11, 1870. The church must have suffered some damage in 1870.

304. Letter from James B. Avirett to Bishop Whittingham, July 26, 1871.

305. Ibid., August 16, 1871.

306. Ibid., February 5, 1872.

307. Ibid., February 21, 1872.

308. Ibid., August 19, 1872.

309. Located on present Kelly Store Road.

310. Anniversary Program: Catoctin United Methodist Church.

311. Interview with Mary Miller Martin, February 18, 1982.

312. Ibid.

313. Interview with Margaret Anders Hoke, November 15, 1981.

314. McPherson, "Recollections of Catoctin Parish."

Chapter 9

315. Frederick County Tax Book 1923, Frederick County Deed 344: 369, cited in Contract Archaeology, Inc., *Historical and Archaeological Survey*, 30.

316. Frederick County Tax Book 1923, Frederick County Deed 360: 90, cited in Contract Archaeology, Inc., *Historical and Archaeological Survey*, 30.

317. Frederick County Tax Book 1923, Frederick County Deed 364: 146, cited in Contract Archaeology, Inc., *Historical and Archaeological Survey*, 30.

318. *Frederick Daily News*, March 19, 1929.

319. Frederick County Deed 414: F587-589, cited in Contract Archaeology, Inc., *Historical and Archaeological Survey*, 30.

320. Frederick County Deed 407: 145, cited in Contract Archaeology, Inc., *Historical and Archaeological Survey*, 30.

321. NCR press release, June 11, 1954, CMP, cited in Kirkconnell, *Catoctin Mountain Park*, 101.

322. Pearre, Letter to the Honorable Russell H. McCain, March 23, 1955.

323. Ernst, Letter to Governor John Tawes, April 13, 1959.

324. *Frederick Post*, February 11, 1965.

325. Professor John Fauth of University College Cortland, New York, suggested these pits were used for limonite and hematite ore for the furnace and that limestone recovered from the pits was used as flux. Fauth, Letter to Catoctin Furnace Historical Society, March 31, 1972.

326. *Sunday Star,* June 20, 1971.

327. Mentzer, "Time and Times of Catoctin Furnace"; *Frederick Post*, March 18, 1972; March 20, 1972; March 21, 1972; March 22, 1972; March 23, 1972; March 24, 1972; March 25, 1972; March 27, 1972; March 28, 1972; March 29, 1972; March 30, 1972; March 31, 1972; April 1, 1972; April 3, 1972; April 5, 1972.

328. *The News*, April 7, 1972.

329. Morton, Letter to Walter Woodford, March 14, 1973; Cantwell, Letter to Mr. Fisher, January 25, 1972.

330. Orr and Orr, *Intensive Archaeological Survey*, 93.

331. Catoctin Furnace Historical Society By-Laws, Article 2, Section 1, 1973.

332. Maryland Department of Natural Resources, *Catoctin Furnace*.

333. *Frederick County Sentinel,* January 9, 1974.

334. Ibid.

335. Ibid.

336. Ibid.

337. Orr and Orr, *Field Report*.

338. Thomas, Mellen, Payne, Burnston and McCarthy, *Archaeological Investigations*; Struthers, *Archaeological Survey*; Burnston and Thomas, *Archaeological Data Recovery*; Reed, *Catoctin Furnace Ironmaster's House*; Parrington and Schenk, *Report on the Excavation*; Reed and Reed, *Catoctin Furnace*.

339. Gustke, "Restoration Project."

340. Gardner, *News-Post*, October 16, 2003.

BIBLIOGRAPHY

PRIMARY RESOURCES

Public Records

Frederick County Equity Records. Frederick County Courthouse, Frederick, Maryland.

Frederick County Land Records. Frederick County Courthouse, Frederick, Maryland.

Frederick County Real Assessment Records. Frederick County Courthouse, Frederick, Maryland.

Frederick County Record of Wills. Frederick County Courthouse, Frederick, Maryland.

Journals of the Continental Congress. Madison Building, Library of Congress, Washington, D.C.

Original Wills. Hall of Records, Annapolis, Maryland.

Papers of the Continental Congress. Microfilm Division, National Archives, Washington, D.C.

Provincial Court Judgment Records. Hall of Records, Annapolis, Maryland.

Provincial Land Office Records. Hall of Records, Annapolis, Maryland.

Revolutionary Records. Agents Letter Book, Hall of Records, Annapolis, Maryland.

Revolutionary War Papers, Series A. Hall of Records, Annapolis, Maryland.

United States Census Records, 1790–1870. Microfilm, C. Burr Artz Library, Frederick, Maryland.

Correspondence

Birnie collection. Hall of Records, Annapolis, Maryland.

Blackford correspondence. Historical Society of Frederick County, Frederick, Maryland.

Letter from James Johnson Jr. to his children, September 1, 1842. Historical Society of Frederick County, Frederick, Maryland.

Letters from Archives of Mount St. Mary's College. Emmitsburg, Maryland.

Letters from Maryland Diocesan Archives. On deposit in Maryland Historical Society, Baltimore, Maryland.

McPherson–Brien Correspondence. Property of C.E. Gardiner, Catoctin Furnace, Thurmont, Maryland.

Ledgers

Catoctin Furnace Ledger 1899–1900. Property of Catoctin Furnace Historical Society, Inc., Thurmont, Maryland.

McPherson Farm Books #1 and #2. Property of C.E. Gardiner, Catoctin Furnace, Thurmont, Maryland.

Diaries

Diaries of Moravian clergy, 1798–1850. Moravian Archives, Bethlehem, Pennsylvania.

Moravian Missionary Letters, 1766–1787. Moravian Archives, Bethlehem, Pennsylvania.

Minutes

All Saints Church Vestry Minutes. All Saints Church, Frederick, Maryland.

Minutes of the Frederick County Board of School Commissioners. Board of Education Office, Frederick, Maryland.

Plats and Maps

Bond, Isaac. *Map of Frederick County*. Baltimore, MD: E Sachse, 1853.

Frederick County Survey Records. Frederick County Courthouse, Frederick, Maryland.

Lake, D.J. *Atlas of Frederick County, Maryland*. Philadelphia: C.O. Titus & Co., 1873.

Plat of Kunkel Property. Frederick County Equity Record #5229, WIP 5:401.

Varle, Charles. *A Map of Frederick & Washington Counties, State of Maryland*. Philadelphia, 1808.

Miscellaneous Records

Convention Journals of the Diocese of Maryland. Maryland Diocesan Archives, on deposit in Maryland Historical Society, Baltimore, Maryland.

Inspection and Survey Record of Public Schools of Frederick County, Maryland. Helfenstein & Urner, Agents, Insurance Company of North America.

Journal and Correspondence of Maryland Council of Safety. Baltimore: Maryland Historical Society, 1893.

Meredith Papers. MS 1367. Maryland Historical Society, Baltimore, Maryland.

National Archives. Microfilm Division. Record Group 93. National Archives, Washington, D.C.

————. M 247. National Archives, Washington, D.C.

Records of Marriages and Burials in the Monocacy Church in Frederick County, Maryland. Translated by Frederick Sheeley Weiser. Washington, D.C.: National Genealogical Society, 1972.

Unpublished

Blackford Family Bible, MDCCXCIII.

Campbell, J.F. *Autobiography of J.F. Campbell.* N.p., n.d.

Interviews

Interview with Josephy and Clara Carbaugh, November 30, 1981.

Interview with Ethel Carbaugh Devilbliss, April 20, 1981.

Interview with Lloyd and Margaret Anders Hoke, November 15, 1981.

Interview with Mary Miller Martin, February 18, 1982.

Interview with Clinton and Josephine Miller, November 15, 1981.

Interview with Roger Penwell, January 30, 1982.

Interview with William Renner, November 4, 1981.

Interviews with Jessie Reed Stitely, October 2, 1981, and January 10, 1982.

Interview with William and Elva Sweeney, November 28, 1981.

Interview with Mabel Fraley Townsend, September 1981.

SECONDARY SOURCES

Alexander, J.H. *Report on the Manufacture of Iron.* Addressed to the Governor of Maryland. Annapolis, MD: Wm. McNeir, 1840.

Andrews, Matthew Page. *History of Maryland Province and State*. Garden City, NY: Doubleday, Doran & Co., Inc., 1929.

Bining, Arthur Cecil. *Pennsylvania Iron Manufacture in the 18ᵗʰ Century*. New York: Augustus M. Kelley. Reprint, 1938.

————. *The Rise of American Economic Life*. New York: Charles Scribner's Sons, 1943.

Bishop, J. Leander. *A History of American Manufacturers from 1608 to 1860*. Philadelphia: Edward Young & Co., 1866.

Blackford, Susan Leigh, comp. *Letters from Lee's Army*. New York: A.S. Barnes & Co., Inc., 1962.

Blackford, W.W. *War Years with Jeb Stuart*. New York: Charles Scribner's Sons, 1946.

Boyer, Peter Price. *The Charcoal Burner*. Cornwall Methodist Church Centennial Booklet, 1970.

Bruce, Kathleen. *Virginia Iron Manufacture in the Slave Era*. New York: Augustus M. Kelley, 1968.

Bushong, Millard K. *Historic Jefferson County*. Boyce, VA: Carr Publishing Co., Inc., 1972.

Campbell, Penelope. *Maryland in Africa*. Urbana: University of Illinois Press, 1971.

Crowl, Philip A. *Maryland During and After the Revolution*. Baltimore, MD: Johns Hopkins Press, 1943.

Cunz, Deiter. *The Maryland Germans*. Princeton, NJ: Princeton University Press, 1964.

Delaplaine, Edward S. *The Life of Thomas Johnson*. New York: Frederick Hitchcock, The Grafton Press, 1927.

————. *Maryland in Law and History*. New York: Vantage Press, 1964.

Fitzhugh, Robert H. *A Fitzhugh Chart*. Fitzhugh Genealogy. Library of Congress.

French, B.F. *History of the Rise and Progress of the Iron Trade of the U.S. From 1621 to 1857*. New York: Wiley and Halstead, 1858.

Gabrill, J. Montgomery. *Leading Events of Maryland History*. Boston: Ginn & Company, 1917.

Grove, William Jarboe. *History of Carrollton Manor*. Frederick: Marken & Bielfeld, Inc., 1928.

Gutheim, Frederick. *The Potomac*. New York: Rinehart & Co., Inc., 1949.

Heiges, George L. *Henry William Stiegel and His Associates*. Lancaster, PA: Rudisill & Co., Inc., 1948.

Helfenstein, Ernest. *History of All Saints Parish in Frederick County, Maryland 1742–1932*. Frederick, MD: Marken & Bielfeld, Inc., 1932.

Hitselberger, Mary Fitzhugh, and John Philip Dorn. *Bridge in Time*. Redwood City, CA: Monocacy Book Co., 1978.

Klees, Fredric. *The Pennsylvania Dutch*. New York: The MacMillan Co., 1950.

Lesley, J.P. *Iron Manufacturer's Guide to the Furnaces, Forges and Rolling Mills of the U.S.* New York: John Wiley, Publishers, 1859.

Lewis, Ronald L. *Coal, Iron and Slaves. Industrial Slavery in Maryland and Virginia, 1715–1865*. Westport, CT: Greenwood Press, 1940.

McSherry, James. *History of Maryland*. Baltimore, MD: The Baltimore Book Co., 1904.

Oerter, Rev. A.L. *The History of Graceham, Frederick County, Maryland*. Bethlehem, PA: Times Publishing Co., 1913.

Richards, Mildred Hoge. *The Kunkel Family of Frederick, Maryland*. Tuscon, AZ, 1954.

Rumsey, James. *A Plan Wherein The Power of Steam Is Fully Shown*. Berkeley, CA, 1788.

———. *A Short Treatise on the Application of Steam*. Philadelphia, 1788.

Scharf, J. Thomas. *History of Maryland*. Hatsboro, PA: Tradition Press, 1967.

———. *History of Western Maryland*. Baltimore, MD: Regional Publishing Co., 1968. Originally published 1882.

Schultz, Edward T. *First Settlements of Germans in Maryland*. Frederick, MD: David H. Smith, 1896.

Seubold, Helen W., and Frank H. Seubold, comps. *Frederick County, Maryland 1800 Census*. Baltimore: Maryland Genealogical Society, Inc., 1977.

Smith, J. Russell. *The Story of Iron and Steel*. New York: D. Appleton & Co., 1929.

Steiner, Bernard C. *History of Education in Maryland*. Washington, D.C.: Government Printing Office, 1894.

———. *Western Maryland in the Revolution*. Baltimore, MD: The Johns Hopkins Press, 1902.

Swank, James M. *History of the Manufacture of Iron in All Ages*. Philadelphia: The American Iron and Steel Association, 1892.

Termin, Peter. *Iron and Steel in Nineteenth Century America*. Cambridge, MA: MIT Press, 1964.

Thurston, Mynna. *James Rumsey: The Inventor of the Steamboat*. Shepherdstown, WV: 1922.

Tracey, Grace Louise. *Notes From the Records of Old Monocacy*. N.p., 1958.

Walker, Joseph E. *Hopewell Village*. Philadelphia: University of Pennsylvania Press, 1966.

Walsh, Richard, and William Lloyd Fox. *Maryland: A History, 1632–1974*. Baltimore: Maryland Historical Society, 1974.

Williams, Thomas J.C. *History of Frederick County, Maryland*. Hagerstown, MD: The Mail Publishing Co., 1910.

———. *History of Washington County, Maryland*. Baltimore, MD: Regional Publishing Co., 1968.

Periodicals

Campbell, Penelope. "Some Notes on Frederick County's Participation in the Maryland Colonization Scheme." *Maryland Historical Magazine* 66, no.1 (Spring 1971): 51–59.

Walker, Joseph E. "A Summer Day at a Charcoal Iron Furnace." U.S. Department of Interior National Park Service.

Pamphlets

Catoctin United Methodist Church. The First Hundred Years, 1877–1977.
Centennial Celebration in Frederick County, Md. June 28, 1876. Frederick, MD: Baughman Brothers, 1879.
McPherson, Louise. *Recollections of Catoctin Parish.* N.p., 1957.
Mechanicstown: Thurmont Bicentennial & Homecoming Program. July 22–July 29, 1951.
Mentzer, J. Frank. "Catoctin Furnace." *Echoes of History* 4, no. 1 (January 1974): 1–7.

Papers

Bastian, Tyler. "Historical & Archaeological Significance of an Abandoned Iron Mine in Cunningham Falls State Park Near Catoctin Furnace, Frederick County, Maryland." Maryland Geological Survey, August 1973.
Thompson, Michael D. "The Iron Industry in Western Maryland." Paper submitted in 1976, West Virginia University, Morgantown, WV.
Waesche, Norman E. "Economic History of Catoctin Furnace." Term paper for American Economic History course, Johns Hopkins University, 1936.

Unpublished Papers

Fraley, F.W. "History of Catoctin Furnace." Unpublished, 1924.
Renner, William. "How Catoctin Furnace Came About." Unpublished, n.d.

Surveys

Contract Archaeology, Inc. *An Historical and Archaeological Survey of Land Affected by the Dualization of U.S. Route 15.* 1971.
John Milner Associates. *Archaeological Survey of Catoctin Furnace, Cunningham Falls State Park and Adjacent Areas.* 1981.
Mid-Atlantic Archaeological Research. *Archaeological Data Recovery at Catoctin Furnace Cemetery.* 1981.
National Heritage Corporation. *A Report on an Historical Survey of Catoctin Iron Furnace & Cunningham Falls State Park.* 1975.
Orr & Son, Consulting Archaeologists. *An Intensive Archaeological Survey of Alignment 1 Corridor.* 1978.

Reports

Biographical Directory of the American Congress, 1774–1771. Washington, D.C.: U.S. Government Printing Office, 1971.

General Frederick County Directory. Frederick, MD: W.T. Delaplaine & Co., 1886.

Maryland: Its Resources, Industries and Institutions. Baltimore, MD: Johns Hopkins University, 1893.

Miller, Charles W., comp. *Post Offices of Frederick County for the Year 1887.* Frederick, MD.

Reed, Douglas C. *Catoctin Furnace Iron Masters House.* Report prepared for Professor John Vlach, George Washington University, December 1981.

Robbins, Michael W. *Maryland's Iron Industry During the Revolutionary War Era.* Report prepared for the Maryland Bicentennial Commission, 1973.

Singewald, Joseph T., Jr. *Report on the Iron Ores of Maryland.* Baltimore, MD: The Johns Hopkins Press, 1911.

State of Maryland Board of Natural Resources, Joseph T. Singewald Jr., director. *The Physical Features of Carroll County and Frederick County.* Baltimore, MD, 1946.

Newspapers

Advertisement. *Frederick Town Herald* 18, no. 45, Saturday, April 1, 1820.

Advertisement. *Frederick Town Herald* 18, no. 46, Saturday, April 8, 1820.

Advertisement. *Frederick Town Herald* 10, nos. 6 & 7, July 13 and 20, 1811.

Advertisement. *Frederick News*, Wednesday, April 18, 1888.

The Citizen, Industrial Edition. Frederick, September 30, 1904.

Dunlap's Maryland Gazette or the Baltimore General Advertiser 3, no. 120, Tuesday, August 12, 1777.

The Examiner. Frederick, Wednesday, September 14, 1853.

Frederick News. "Foundries of Frederick Town Subject of Seminar." May 21, 1956.

Frederick Post. "The Time and Times of Catoctin Furnace." March 18, 1972–April 4, 1972.

Frederick Town Herald 9, no. 46, April 20, 1811.

The Hornet. Fredericktown, Maryland, January 16, 1811.

Mentzer, Frank. "The Spirit of Catoctin." *Catoctin Enterprize*, May 23, 1969.

Waynesboro Herald, August 21, 1940.

Miscellaneous

Transactions of the Moravian Historical Society 9. Nazareth, MD: Whitfield House, 1913.

INDEX

INDEX

N

National Register of Historic Places nomination 99

O

ore pits 55

P

Potomac Hills Development Company 96
preservation efforts 103
private schools 80
public schools 84

R

Rawlings, John 18, 63, 68
restoration projects 103

S

Sharp, Earnest and Willa 44
slave cemetery 67
slavery 66
Springfield 18, 19, 20, 65
Stoney Park 11, 13, 20

T

Thornburgh, Thomas 20
Thropp, Joseph 47, 62, 95, 96
Trexler, Oscar 95

V

Vertrees, John 9, 11, 12, 85, 105

W

Waesche, L.R. 41, 42, 56, 109, 110, 122
Western Maryland Railroad 45, 56, 93, 95, 110
Wetzel, Hans 11
women's labor 79
worker entertainment 78

ABOUT THE AUTHOR

E lizabeth Yourtee Anderson (1926–2011) was awarded a BA in history from Hood College and graduated cum laude with departmental honors. She was a local historian specializing in the history of Catoctin Furnace and the early iron-making industry of central and western Maryland. She was a founding member of the Catoctin Furnace Historical Society, Inc., and served as an officer until her death in 2011. She was a member of the Thurmont Historical Society and numerous other local, state and national historic preservation and history organizations. She was also the author of *Faith in the Furnace*, a history of Harriet Chapel in Catoctin Furnace, Maryland; served as editor of *The Chimes*; and presented numerous talks about the history of the Catoctin Furnace area to state and local historical societies, site visitors and dignitaries.